D0098249

Praise for *eBoot Camp: Proven Internet Marketing Techniques to Grow Your Business*

"Good tools, good book, good reading!"
—Michael Gerber, author of the #1 *NY Times* bestseller *The E-Myth Revisited*

"Understanding how to do business on the Internet is an essential part of business today. *eBoot Camp* is packed with low cost, easy-to-implement strategies that will help boost your search engine ranking and drive traffic to your web site. Every small business owner and entrepreneur should own a copy."
—T. Harv Eker, author of the #1 *NY Times* bestseller *Secrets of the Millionaire Mind*

"Do you want to ignite your sales and drastically increase profits through the Internet? This is the first book that gives practical, easy-to-follow action steps proven to increase traffic to your web site. You'll think Corey Perlman wrote *eBoot Camp* just for you."
—Sharon Lechter, Member of the President's Advisory Council on Financial Literacy, International bestselling author, co-author of *Three Feet from Gold* with The Napoleon Hill Foundation

"Corey Perlman has written a great primer on using technology to market effectively. *eBoot Camp* provides a complete overview that is easy to understand and easy to implement. Read this book for a quick and concise game plan for using the Internet to grow your business."
—Mark Sanborn, President, Sanborn & Associates, Inc., bestselling author of *The Fred Factor, You Don't Need a Title to be a Leader* and *The Encore Effect*

"Similar to what I teach in my 'Mind Capture' book series, Corey makes the often confusing and contradictory world of online marketing simple and easy for people to not only learn about, but more importantly use and implement within their business. This book is the perfect blueprint for any new or existing business owner looking to avoid hype and expensive strategies to help them quickly and cost effectively improve their web-based marketing efforts. Kudos to Corey for sharing his years of knowledge, strategies, and teachings within this growing and ever changing medium!"

—Tony Rubleski, President, Mind Capture Group and #1 bestselling author (www.MindCaptureBook.com)

"By implementing the concepts from this book, we have increased our Internet leads by more than 400 percent—which ranked highest among a benchmark group of the largest Dale Carnegie franchises in the world. A must-read for any franchisee or small business owner."

—John Rodgers, Dale Carnegie Training Franchisee

"The first time I read *eBoot Camp,* I stayed up until 4 am implementing the strategies the book suggested. The next day, I had a blog, a LinkedIn page and an article live and published online. Corey gives his Internet marketing secrets away and provides step-by-step instructions on how to get it all accomplished. If you're looking to get more business from the Web and don't know where to begin, stop everything else you're doing and read this book."

—Ralph Mark Maupin, Managing Member, Right Now Marketing Group, LLC

"My wife and I wrote a book together and wanted to increase sales through our web site. Two months after we implemented the strategies from *eBoot Camp,* our book sales doubled! We knew very little about Internet marketing, but this book provided step-by-step instructions to guide us through the process. This is a must-read for anyone looking to boost sales through the Internet."

—Jared Massanari (BuildingaHouseTogether.com)

"Having recently opened my business, I was overwhelmed with what needed to get done. I knew the Internet would be critical to the success of my business, but I didn't know where to start. The techniques in *eBoot Camp* gave me a roadmap to exactly what I needed to do and how to do it. In just a few weeks, I launched a web site, and I already have a top Google ranking! Thank you so much, Corey!"

—Jaime White, Core Sports Pilates, Plymouth, MI

eBOOT CAMP

eBOOT CAMP

**PROVEN
INTERNET
MARKETING
TECHNIQUES
TO GROW YOUR
BUSINESS**

Corey Perlman

WILEY

John Wiley & Sons, Inc

Published by John Wiley & Sons, Inc., Hoboken, New Jersey
Published simultaneously in Canada

For general information on our other products and services or for technical support, please
contact our Customer Care Department within the United States at (800) 762-2974, outside
the United States at (317) 572-3993 or fax (317) 572-4002.

Wiley also publishes its books in a variety of electronic formats. Some content that appears
in print may not be available in electronic books. For more information about Wiley products,
visit our web site at www.wiley.com.

Library of Congress Cataloging-in-Publication Data:

Perlman, Corey, 1978-
    eBoot camp : proven Internet marketing techniques to grow your business / Corey
Perlman.
      p. cm.
    Includes index.
    ISBN 978-0-470-41159-9 (cloth)
      1. Internet marketing. I. Title. II. Title: eBoot camp.
HF5415.1265.P47 2008
  658.8'72—dc22
                                                                2008034574

Printed in the United States of America

10 9 8 7 6 5 4 3 2 1

My Mom
Whom I miss each and every day

My Wife
To whom I thank God for each and every day

The Small Business Owner
Whom I respect and admire

CONTENTS

SECTION 2
Create a Web Presence to Dominate the Search Engines and Drastically Increase Traffic to Your Web Site.

ACKNOWLEDGMENTS

As with any major project, it's a collective effort to go from exciting idea to mission accomplished.

Thank you to my wife, Jessica, for your love and support and for being my sounding board for this book. Thank you, Dad and Kate, for being my cheering section and constant nurturers. Jaime, my brother, thank you for your love and encouragement throughout this journey.

This book would never have existed without my friend and mentor, Dr. Dale Brill. Dale, you will always be the original eBoot Camp drill sergeant.

Thank you to my dear friend John Marcus, my editor. John, without you the whole world would know what a terrible speller I am. You earned that John's Pizza slice!

I want to thank Robert Wilson, my agent, for helping lead the way to getting the book published.

Thank you to Shannon and the team at John Wiley and Sons for putting together a beautiful book. You were all an absolute pleasure to work with.

Then there's the cast of people who I surround myself with that fuel my creative fire with encouragement, love, and support. Thank you to Joe "Partner!" Hart for helping me stay personally, professionally, and spiritually aligned.

To DJ Brown, my old friend, I thank for your commitment to our friendship and never letting me get too far away from where I came from.

To the original eBoot Campers, Clint, Ellie, Raina, Jenny, and Tara, thank you for being a part of this book's foundation.

I owe a big debt of gratitude to my friend, Bill Crawford, who volunteered countless times to make the first eBoot Camps a success.

Finally, thank you to Bob, Liz, Eric, Theresia, Julie, Jerry, and Tim, my accountability group, who would not let me stop writing.

INTRODUCTION

Background

So what do a plumber, author, psychotherapist, and steel-drum player all have in common? They each knew that the Internet was the key to unlocking more customers for their business but they didn't have the slightest idea how to do it or where to begin. The only thing they were sure of is that they didn't have a lot of time or money to spend in finding the answer. And every single one has

since been transformed from a self-proclaimed computer novice into a full-fledged Internet Marketing Superhero!

Each of these individuals has developed an Internet marketing skill set so powerful that they can compete for Internet traffic with any business—no matter how big or small. They no longer feel daunted by the vast landscape of the Internet and know just enough to be an effective and powerful Internet marketer.

You, too, will don the red cape and nerdy glasses once you've finished this book. (Please send me your photo!) All it takes is an open mind and some good, ol'-fashioned enthusiasm to put these techniques to use.

And I promise that you don't need to be a computer whiz in order to successfully market your business online. Anyone can do this, and I'm a true testament to that. Back in high school, my computer science teacher generously gave me a C-minus, one point above failing, and left me with the advice that it's better to be lucky than good. Thanks, Mr. Dunkin!

With Mr. Dunkin's words still ringing in my ear, I enrolled at Florida State University and continued to struggle through my marketing classes. I did survive four years of undergraduate work and three years of graduate work and I was now the proud owner of a Master's degree and some hefty student loans. Now I just needed this luck thing to land me a good job out of college so I could pay for those loans! Wouldn't you know it, my professor and mentor, Dale Brill, invited me to join him on a project with the eCommerce division of General Motors (eGM).

eGM asked us to conduct a series of one-day seminars to their dealership personnel about the world of Internet marketing. We called these seminars "eBoot Camps" because of the vast amount of e-commerce information we were covering in such a short period of time. I was a nervous wreck because now I was expected to teach on a subject I still didn't quite understand. Nevertheless, we headed out in an eight-passenger van, canvassing the country in just four short months.

We certainly had our work cut out for us as the GM folks were a crowd with short attention spans and no-nonsense attitudes. We needed to find a way to cut through the technical jargon and create a presentation in layman's terms that answered the question: How can I start using the Internet to drive sales and increase revenue?

We developed an action-packed presentation crammed with so much value that, as the word of the seminars spread, our venues began to sell out. And before we had a chance to catch our breath, our lead instructor was being interviewed by both the *Wall Street Journal* and *Fast Company*. Toward the end of the tour, I began teaching parts of the sessions and, wouldn't you know it, this Internet marketing stuff finally sank in.

Unfortunately Mr. Dunkin failed to tell me the part about how luck has a way of turning on a dime. Our tour ended as abruptly as it began when the events of September 11, 2001 took place. On the brink of taking the tour overseas and creating a global phenomenon, we were shut down, and the GM eBoot Camp was over.

I soon left General Motors and started a career in the eLearning field. I went from one of the largest companies in the world to a tiny one with only about five employees. I was instantly addicted to the world of small business and knew that was where I wanted to spend the rest of my professional career. Our company survived the dot-bomb era, and we ended up selling the company in 2005.

So now what? I needed that luck thing to strike again, but it just wasn't happening. That was until I ran into some friends who ran seminars for real estate investors. They wanted to do an Internet marketing seminar but did not have a resident expert on hand. I jumped at the chance to teach again. The old eBoot Camp material needed a complete overhaul as it was dated and had a completely different audience. But I was excited to bring it back to life.

The new eBoot Camp was a complete success, and we ran one after another, selling out each venue along the way. I started getting requests to run eBoot camps for all sorts of professions. Each time, I revamped the material to make it relevant for that audience. We created Internet marketing superstars out of all kinds of people, from a 29-year-old physical therapist to a 64-year-old real estate agent. Eventually, the material was made broad enough to reach every audience, no matter the profession.

We were now teaching 30 to 60 business owners at a time, but I felt we could increase that number exponentially. My goal was to take the magic that was created in the classroom and bottle it in a book. And that brings us to the journey on which you're about to embark.

Although you may have sensed some sarcasm in the luck references above, I do feel very lucky to be able to do what I love to do. This book marries my three passions: small business, Internet marketing, and helping people. So thank you, Mr. Dunkin, for teaching me that it is better to be lucky than good and, most important, that proving your doubters wrong can be the ultimate motivator.

This Book

No matter what type of business you're in, you must have an effective, user-friendly web site and a powerful search engine presence to be able to thrive in today's complex and competitive marketplace. When you've finished reading this book, you'll have created concrete action plans that you can implement to dramatically improve your search engine rankings, increase traffic to your web site, and grow your business.

This book does not teach you how to become a programmer so you can create a web site or change your existing one. I promised results with limited time and money, and designing web sites takes a long time to master. Leave the developing to the experts and spend your time where it's most needed: creating online content that will result in more people visiting your web site and becoming your customers.

This book is written in layman's terms, and all the "techie" language that you need to know has been clearly defined and translated. You will no longer feel like your web designer speaks another language. For example, the next time a designer tells you how many "hits" you have, ask if he's referring to "hits," "page views," or "unique visitors," since they all mean different things. He'll know he's not dealing with an Internet novice anymore.

The bottom line is this book was written for anyone, regardless of their Internet or marketing experience. The only requirements are an open mind and an Internet connection. I never liked when people spoke over my head and made things more complicated than they needed to be. My intention is for this book to make complete sense to the Internet novice. If by the end of this book you have a question that is unanswered, you can ask your question at ebootcampquestion.com, and I will do my best to get you an answer.

In every workshop I run, there are always at least two or three people who are very knowledgeable about the Internet or Internet marketing. They come in handy when questions are asked that I don't know the answer to. They also always say that they still learned many useful techniques and tips in the workshop that they can use in their business. So to all my already super-techy geeks, this book is also for you.

Your Web Site

Your web site is the foundation of your Internet marketing campaign and a crucial element in everything we'll be discussing in this book. After all, your web site is your virtual store, and it must be nurtured and maintained just as you do with your business. When you complete this book, there will be changes you'll want to make to your web site. Some will be visible to users while others will pertain to information geared toward the search engines. You'll also create additional online resources to open new doors so traffic will visit your site.

I've dedicated the final chapter of this book to the subject of web site usability and design; this is to help you end up with an attractive, user-friendly site that communicates your products, services, and other information about your business in a clear and concise way.

You'll need the help of your web designer, or the person who currently manages your web site, to implement some of the changes you'll want to make. Even if he or she charges you a small fee ($50–$250 is what I consider small), it will be well worth it. If you don't have someone managing your site or you don't currently have a web site, ask for recommendations from people you know who have web sites you admire.

In closing, your web site probably won't contain all of the features discussed in this book. You might wonder why your web designer didn't explain the different steps you can take to maximize the number of visitors to your site. Although some designers do discuss these matters with their clients, they do lie outside his or her primary job, which is no more than to design a great site for you. These matters are, however, the job and very purpose of this book. In the pages that follow, you'll learn everything you need to know to make your web site search engine friendly and prepare it for a drastic increase in Internet traffic.

It's time to get started.

HOW TO READ THIS BOOK

Each chapter discusses a crucial element of Internet marketing. The discussion is followed by these sections: Tips for Success, Walkthrough, Exercise, Case Study, Resources, Web Tidbits and Cocktail Information, which will help to reinforce the topic under consideration. The sections are described in detail below.

Tips for Success

These are bulleted items of helpful hints, shortcuts, or warnings about the topic being discussed. With 10 years of field experience in Internet marketing, I'll be giving you my secrets—not just on *what to do* to get the results you want, but also on *how to do them effectively, efficiently, and ethically.*

Walkthrough and Exercise

These two sections are the heart and soul of this book.

The walkthrough section is your first opportunity to take a break from reading and go right to your computer. Here, you'll be taken step-by-step through a process to gain a better understanding of the chapter under discussion. I'm a firm believer that action breeds retention, so you'll be given activities to perform throughout the book.

The exercise section is where you'll begin creating your own template for your Internet marketing campaign. Once you've completed this book, you will have created a complete set of meta tags, new homepage content, a blog, press release, e-newsletter template, and much more. Make sure you have a pen or pencil handy at all times.

Case Study

These are real-world examples of people or companies that I've worked with and where I've used these techniques to improve search-engine rankings or drive more traffic to a web site.

Resources

Each chapter provides links to web sites that I've found helpful when working in that area. The link might take you to an article or free tool or a web site that I personally use. I recognize that some of these web sites are quite long and might be tough to copy to a web browser, so I'll have them all available (plus more!) at my web site: ebootcampbook.com/resources.

Cocktail Information

These are facts about Internet marketing that may not help you with your business but will get you major cool points with your friends, family, and coworkers. Imagine being at a company picnic and someone mentions that one terabyte is 1024 megabytes and you calmly interject that it's actually 1024 gigabytes. You'll be the life of the party! These types of conversations happen at your parties too, right?

Web Tidbit

There's only so much content one can fit into a book. I've provided some further information available on the Web.

A final word. Many web sites included in this book begin with "www," such as www.google.com. To avoid constant repetition of these letters, they've been omitted from all web sites that appear in this book.

HOW TO PLAY (AND WIN!) THE SEARCH ENGINE GAME

INTRODUCTION

I enjoy gambling. There's nothing like taking off for a weekend trip to Las Vegas with a bunch of friends. The negative to Sin City is the likely chance you'll come home with empty pockets. You always see people arriving in Las Vegas with a big smile on their face and high expectations for winning, only to see those same faces heading out of town a few days later with bags under their eyes and only a half a sandwich left to their name.

Ah, if there were only a way to swing the odds in our favor. Not by cheating, of course, but by understanding the games so well that we would have an honest edge over the house. Then Las Vegas would truly be a grown-ups' paradise.

At this point you might be wondering if you mistakenly picked up the wrong book. No, no, this is indeed the book you want; I'm just a sucker for a good analogy.

Getting your web site to the top of search engines can sometimes be as frustrating as gambling; you may think you have the game mastered, but still come up empty-handed. You could create an exact replica of a highly ranked web site and yours might not even appear on the search engines. It's not an exact science, and it can drive even the best Internet marketers to the brink of insanity.

But, unlike those Vegas slots, you can stack the odds in your favor and get a leg up on your competition. Master the search engine game and, over time, the odds seem to always find a way to favor the skilled Internet marketer. By following the principles outlined in this section, you can master this game without spending a ton of money or wasting your most precious asset as a business owner: time.

This section, and this entire book for that matter, is about providing you with multiple strategies that will directly impact your search engine rankings. Some may carry more weight than others, but they are all essential pieces to the puzzle. I mentioned earlier that there could be two exact replica web sites and one might appear at the top of Google on a particular search and the other might not even show up. That's because the ranked web site is implementing many of the strategies outlined in this book and the poorly ranked site is counting solely on the content of its site. To the naked eye, you wouldn't notice a difference. But behind the scenes, the two sites could not be more different.

This section will focus mostly on the *organic searches*, the free ones, but Chapter 2 will give you what you need to use *paid searches* (sponsored ads) in your Internet marketing campaign. You'll learn the differences between the two and which one I prefer in Chapter 1.

A question I often hear is whether or not you should pay Search Engine Optimization (SEO) companies to do this work for you. If you have the budget, most companies do a good job of getting your web site higher in the search engines. The critical factor of having success working with an SEO company is your involvement. You must be a part of the process in order for it to be effective. Any good SEO company would agree with me. That's why, regardless if you choose to do this work yourself or hire a company to do it for you, you still need to read this book.

As an example, you will create the list of words that search engines evaluate when deciding where to rank your web site. Who knows those words better than you? The majority of the information that needs to be created can come only from you. No one understands your business or your customers better than you do. I'll be providing the framework and all the blanks you need to fill in, but only you know the exact words that can truly make an impact on the search engines and, as a result, an impact on your bottom line.

CHAPTER 1

ANATOMY OF A SEARCH ENGINE

The difference between organic and paid searches and where you should focus your time and resources.

Before we delve into how to win the search engine game, let's first go over the basics of what search engines are, how they work, and who the major players are.

Search engines are tools that inventory content on the Web based on criteria that the searcher is looking for. That content can be in the form of a web page, video, picture, or other online resource. When search engines evaluate a web page, they may take into account many aspects, including the domain name (also known as the web site address), the web site's content and its meta tags. Meta tags are content you create specifically for search engines to help them decipher what your web site is about and where to place your site in their search results. Meta tags are located in the source code (programming language) of your web site. The components that make up your meta tags will be discussed in detail later in this book.

To view any web site's meta tags, you just need to look in the source code of that web site. To do this in Internet Explorer, simply click on "View" from the top navigation bar and then click on "Source" in the drop-down box. I like to review the top Google results in my industry and take a look at their web site's meta

Example of a web site's source code.

```
www.investorteams[1] - Notepad

File  Edit  Format  View  Help

<html>
<head>
<title>Investor Teams. Find Your Team. Find Your Way.</title>
<meta http-equiv="Content-Type" content="text/html; charset=iso-8859-1">
<meta name="keywords" content="investor, investor teams, investor resources, investing, investments, real estate, taxes, stoc
<meta name="description" content="A free site for investors to find educational resources and the right people to make up the
<link href="css.css" rel="stylesheet" type="text/css">
</head>

<body bgcolor="#003366" leftmargin="0" topmargin="0" marginwidth="0" marginheight="0">

<table width="100%" border="0" cellspacing="0" cellpadding="5">
    <td align="center"><table width="768" border="0" cellspacing="0" cellpadding="0">
        <tr>
            <td><table width="100%" border="0" cellspacing="0" cellpadding="0">
                <tr>
                    <td><table width="100%" border="0" cellspacing="0" cellpadding="0">
                        <tr>
                            <td><img src="images/header/leftPanel.jpg" alt="Investor Teams" width="533" height="133"></td>

                            <td align="left"><img src="images/header/rtPanel.jpg" width="235" height="133" border="0" usemap="#Map4

                        </tr>
                    </table></td>
                </tr>
                <tr>
                    <td><table width="100%" border="0" cellspacing="0" cellpadding="0">
                        <tr>




                            <td bgcolor="003366"><img src="images/spacer.gif" width="1" height="10"></td>
```

tags. If they are at the top, they most likely have an excellent set of meta tags.

There are three types of search engines: crawlers (or spiders), human powered, and a hybrid of the two. Google.com is an example of a crawler, and ChaCha.com is a human-powered search engine. The difference between these engines is simply how they evaluate web sites for placement. The crawlers use software to perform searches, and human-powered engines use actual people to evaluate the web sites. MSN.com is an example of a hybrid search engine that uses both spiders and humans to evaluate web sites.

As explained in the introduction, there are two types of search engine results, paid and organic. The organic are the free searches that come up on the left side of a search engine, and paid searches (also known as sponsored links) show up on the right side, and sometimes even above the organic searches. I'll dive deeper into paid searches in the next chapter.

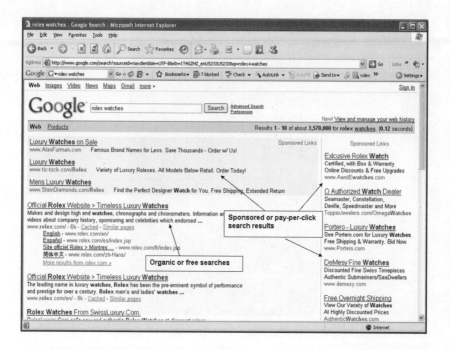

I'm often asked which type of search I prefer: organic or sponsored links. I spend most of my time working on my organic results, although I do not discount the importance of using sponsored links as part of your Internet marketing campaign. Research proves that people still focus their attention primarily on the top organic searches before they review the sponsored results. Part of the reason for this is search engine users are concerned about the substance of the sites that came up on the sponsored results. With sponsored searches, people pay to have their web site show up in the search results as opposed to organic, where results are displayed purely by the relevance to the words that were typed in the search box.

Take a look at the following picture. It's a heat map that tracks where people's eyes go as soon as they arrive at google.com. The brighter colors indicate where the majority of the searchers are looking. As you can see, the vast majority of the colors are over the organic search results and not on the sponsored links on the right side of the page. Also note the vast difference in coming up on the top of Google versus the bottom.

Source: Google Heat Map provided by eyetools.com

With organic results, people are more likely to gain the information they're looking for. More importantly, the organic searches are free, so you can win the search engine game the old-fashioned way, and put those marketing dollars back into your pocket.

With all that said, I have many friends who are making a great living by solely using sponsored links to sell their products and services. Although the majority of the first section of this book will focus on organic searches, I'll give you everything you need to effectively use sponsored links in the next chapter.

There are hundreds of search engines on the Internet, but only a few dominate the search landscape. The graphic below displays the U.S. market share of the top search engines in the world in March 2008. Those are the ones you want to focus on when implementing the strategies outlined in this section. The good news is if you are seeing positive results on the largest search engines, it's highly probable you will see similar results on the smaller ones.

Here are the major search engines that you'll want to focus your efforts on:

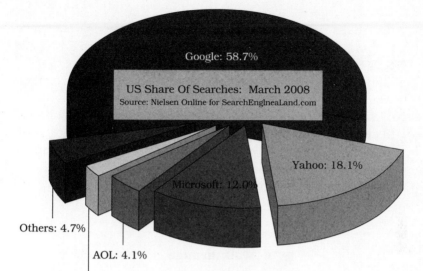

Google (the proverbial 800-pound gorilla)
Yahoo
MSN
AOL
Ask

As a review, here are the different types of search engines along with an example of each:

- Crawler-powered: Automated software that visits a web site and looks for keywords and meta tags, such as Google.
- Human-powered: People submit information that is indexed and cataloged, such as ChaCha.
- Hybrid: Uses both automated software and human interaction to create search results, such as MSN.

Tips for Success

No. 1. Make sure your web designer has a firm grasp on the importance of making your web site search engine friendly. The litmus test question is "How important is it to create meta tags for my web site?" If they don't say "very important," then I'd consider finding another web designer.

No. 2. Review web sites that you always see at the top of Google. As you learn more about how search engines rank web sites, you'll begin to see patterns that each of these web sites use.

No. 3. When updates are made to your web site, you should alert each of the major search engines to reevaluate your site. When you've completed this book, you'll want to perform this task. See the exercise below for instructions on how to do this on google.com.

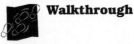 **Walkthrough**

Step 1. Open your browser and go to eBootCampbook.com.

Step 2. Click on "View" from the navigation bar at the top of your page.

Step 3. Click on "Source" if using Internet Explorer or click on "Page Source" if using Mozilla Firefox.

Step 4. Find the site's meta tags, which include the keywords, title tag, and meta description tag.

You now know where to look when evaluating other web sites' meta tags, and this can come in handy as you start to develop your own meta tags.

 Exercise (To be performed once you've finished reading this book)

Step 1. Go to google.com/addurl.

Step 2. Add your web site so that Google will know you're ready for them to evaluate your site. (This is a free service.)

Step 3. Repeat this process at Yahoo!, MSN, AOL and Ask.com.

Resources

Searchenginewatch.com provides the latest news on search engines.

Google.com/support/webmasters/bin/answer.py? answer=35291 is Google's take on search-engine optimization companies.

Highrankings.com/forum/ is a forum for people to discuss search-engine optimization strategies.

Seochat.com provides more articles and information about search engine optimization.

Cocktail Information

Dogpile.com is a meta search engine. It searches other engines, such as Google, Yahoo, MSN and Ask, and so on, and comes up with results based on the ranking of web sites across all the other search engines. This unique process can provide a higher frequency of relevant results during a targeted search. Give it a try!

CHAPTER 2

PAY-PER-CLICK (SPONSORED ADS)

Used the right way, paying for placement on Google and other search engines can be a powerful way to market your business.

I recently read a fantastic book by Chris Anderson entitled *The Long Tail*. He explains a phenomenon that is currently taking place where, since the dawn of the Internet, the big players in each industry are losing their market share to the thousands (and sometimes millions) of regular people like you and me. Sites like Amazon.com have unlimited shelf space and enable millions of unknown authors to share the same stage as world famous authors like John Grisham or Stephen King.

Anderson explains the advertising industry has experienced the same type of transformation thanks to a certain search engine called—yep, you guessed it—Google!

Google Adwords (the name Google gives its sponsored ads program) has made it simple for a small town sandwich shop to advertise against the likes of Panera Bread, Subway, or Cosi. And thanks to the use of keywords (words that your potential customers would use to search in Google) you can localize your advertising far better than any offline advertising campaign.

This same functionality works on the next two largest search engines in the world: Yahoo! and MSN. I'll continue to use Google as my search engine example of choice, but this information is applicable to Yahoo! and MSN as well.

Here's how it works. When a person searches for a word or phrase in Google, you can pay to be included in the results that are shown (see graphic below for areas Google designates for sponsored ads). You are only charged if the searcher actually clicks on your sponsored link, not just if your ad appears. You may have heard of the phrase "pay-per-click" or "cost-per-click" and both are commonly used when discussing Google Adwords. Pay-per-click means you only are charged when someone clicks on your ad, and cost-per-click is how much you are charged when someone clicks on your ad.

So how much does it cost to pay for a sponsored ad on Google? Well, it depends on the keywords that you want your ad to show up on. Google will give you an estimate of what the "cost-per-click" will be for the keywords you want to use.

Let's say you own a golf club shop in Phoenix, Arizona, and you want to pay to come up in Google when someone searches "golf clubs Phoenix." If you used Google Adword's estimating tool, it might tell you that it will cost you between $0.69 and $0.96 cents each time a person clicks on your ad. The tool will also give you an estimate of the position you might come up in. You can then provide Google a budget of what you are willing to spend each month. So let's say for the above keywords, you only want to pay $100 a month to have your ad show up on Google. After roughly 100–150 people clicked on your sponsored link, Google would stop your ad from showing up on the sponsored results for the rest of the day. This is a very helpful feature to ensure business owners don't blow past their marketing budgets in a single day.

If you are going to use sponsored links, my suggestion is to focus on specific keyword phrases as appose to generic, broad phrases. Your dollar will go further, and your traffic will be more targeted. Let's use the Phoenix golf club shop again as our example. I would rather pay the $0.69 cents per click for the phrase "golf clubs Phoenix" than let's say $1.60 for the phrase "golf club store" or "golf store." Even if I did come up on those search results, the searcher could be from anywhere in the world. Yes, some people will buy clubs online, but most are like me and want to "kick the tires" before they buy.

Once you've decided on the keywords that you want your ad to appear on Google and the budget you are willing to spend, you then have to decide on the content for your ad. As seen below, you are given space for a title (a blue link that users can click on) and sub-title (the black text after the blue link), and you have control as to what those two sentences say. You need to be descriptive and let the searcher know exactly who you are and what products and services you have to offer, and you also need to sell them on why they should pick your link over all the others. If you find that your ad is not getting the traffic you were hoping for, you should consider altering your title and subtitle in hopes for better results.

You've heard me say that I prefer to use the organic (or free) side of Google.com to advertise my products and services as opposed to paying for my results. Although I stand by that statement, I still use sponsored links as a way to drive traffic to my site. When I use them, I use pinpoint accuracy when coming up with the keyword phrases and, therefore, I only get qualified customers looking for my information. I also use the help of keyword suggestion tools to help me find other good keywords for my campaign. Google has its own keyword suggestion tool and that link is listed below in the resource section.

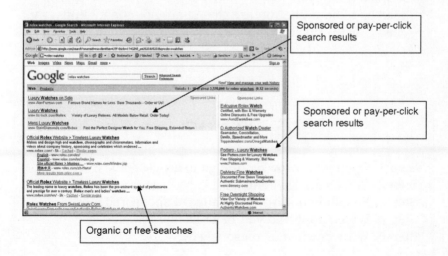

Sponsored ads are a very effective way to deliver traffic to your web site, but you must be patient and not be afraid to alter your campaign when necessary. If you are not getting the results you are looking for, choose different keywords or alter your ad copy. And don't worry, after you finish the rest of this book, you'll be enjoying great success with your organic search results, and the sponsored links will just be icing on the cake.

Tips for Success

No. 1. When using sponsored ads, be creative and use uncommon words. This will cost less, and you'll get more bang for your buck. Popular words can be quite costly because each time a user clicks on your link, you get charged.

No. 2. When using paid searches, you can also request that your web site NOT come up when certain words are used. For example, many people who use sponsored links request that when the word "free" is searched, their site be omitted from the search results. They know the user is searching for free information and is likely not to make a purchase on their site.

No. 3. Make adjustments. If you're not getting traffic to your web site, or if the traffic you are getting are not quality leads, try changing the title or subtitle or try using different keywords.

 Walkthrough

Step 1. Open your browser and go to google.com.
Step 2. Search for "golf clubs".
Step 3. You should see a wide range of sponsored ads.
Step 4. Which ad would you most likely click on?
Step 5. Write down your reasons why.

Exercise

Step 1. Create the title for your sponsored ad. Remember, this is the blue link that people click on, and you only are allowed three to five words.

Example: DVD Internet Marketing

Step 2. Come up with your subtitle. This is the black text below the blue link, and you are allowed about 10 to 12 words. This is where you need to sell!

Example: Gain new customers and repeat business through the Web.

Step 3. Add your domain name to the bottom of your campaign.

Example: www.ebootcampbook.com

Step 4. Come up with a budget per month that you are willing to spend for sponsored ads.

Example: $100

Resources

adwords.google.com is where to go to advertise on google.com.

searchmarketing.yahoo.com is where to go to advertise on Yahoo!.

adcenter.microsoft.com is where to go to advertise on MSN.com. https://adwords.Google.com/select/KeywordTool External is Google's keyword suggestion tool.

Cocktail Information

So it's probably safe to say that online advertising has not just made a dent in the advertising market, but a crater-sized hole. Here are some staggering statistics about the growth of online advertising:

Online advertising revenues are expected to double in two years (2010) to $80 billion. (Source: http://www.npr.org/templates/story/story.php?storyId=18615517)

Internet ad spending is expected to exceed 10 percent of global ad investment in 2008 for the first time ever. (Source: mediabuyerplanner.com 2007.)

Search will comprise 65–70 percent measured online advertising in 2008, up from 50 percent in 2005. (Source: mediabuyerplanner.com 2007.)

In 2004, Google went public at around $85 a share. In four years, it has skyrocketed as high as $700 a share—doubling three times over.

DOMAIN NAMES AND ALTERNATE DOMAIN NAMES

Own the right web site addresses and watch your traffic soar!

In this chapter, you will learn:

The characteristics of a domain name.

The different types of extensions (.com, .net) and which you
should own.

How to search for and buy domain names.

How to capture "guess and go" traffic by owning alternate
domain names.

How to find out who owns a domain name and when it is
scheduled to expire.

Author's note: If you already own a domain name, this chapter is still important to read because it explains the value of owning multiple, also known as alternative, domain names.

Your domain name is your web site address or, as I like to call it, your "virtual storefront." It consists of the name of your web site and its extension. Starbucks.com, ebay.com, and att.net are examples of domain names.

The most common extension for a domain name is, of course, .com. But there are many other top-level domains, known as TLDs, that are also available.

The extensions .com, .edu, .gov, .int, .mil, .net, and .org were all created in the 1980s. Then .biz, .info, .name and others appeared

25

in 2001. Although there are many top-level domain names, only a handful—.com, .net, .info, .biz, and .name—are widely used and without restriction.

Another type of extension for domain names is called a "country code." These are two-letter extensions that represent a particular country. Country codes such as .uk (the United Kingdom), .us (the United States) and .tv (Tuvalu) are available to the public, while most others can be used only by those who live in that country.

With so many domain extensions available, which should you choose for your web site? Well, let's eliminate some right off the bat. The extension .gov is reserved for government entities, and .edu can be used only by universities and other educational institutions. You should use .org only if you're a not-for-profit organization, and I'd suggest .tv only if you're in the entertainment business. Some of the other, newer extensions, such as .name or .info, just have not caught on yet. So we are left with .net and .biz as alternatives to .com.

People ask me all the time if .net or .biz are acceptable alternatives if the .com they want is already taken. I liken this situation to owning an imitation Burberry purse or Rolex watch. They look and feel the same, but a .com they are not. If someone goes online and tries to guess what your web site is (this process is known as "guess and go"), they'll most likely guess that it ends in .com. There are exceptions, however, where I'd recommend using a .net. For example, if the .com of your book title is taken or if your only .com options are too long, then I'd recommend using .net or .biz. Also, if you already own the .com name, then I strongly recommend owning the .net and .biz extensions as well, just to ensure that no one else can buy them.

As mentioned earlier, using search engines is the primary way people find web sites. However, a large number of people use the guess-and-go method, where they literally guess what a web site might be and then go for it. For example, let's say you're looking for a Ford dealership in Tampa, Florida. You might jump online and type in tampaford.com. If a Tampa Ford dealership owned that domain and the dealership wasn't too far away, you'd probably head over when you were ready to take a test drive. Even though it's likely that there are multiple Ford dealerships in that city, the person who owns tampaford.com will have just won you as a customer, simply because they owned the right domain. By the way, upon my search of that domain, it doesn't seem an actual dealership owns Tampaford.com. Too bad!

By owning multiple, or alternate, domains, it increases the chances of someone guessing a domain and finding your web site. Let's again use the example of owning a Ford dealership in Tampa. Tampabayford.com might be your domain name, but you might also own stpeteford.com (a neighboring city) and tampafloridaford.com as your alternate domain names. They would all point to your main web site, and you would just advertise tampabayford.com to the public. If someone guessed stpeteford.com or tampafloridaford.com, they would seamlessly be sent to tampabayford.com and would never know the difference. To clarify, you would NOT have three different web sites for each of these domains. All of your domain names would be directed to your single web site.

Your domain name is also an important factor when it comes to search engine rankings. Search engines take notice when your keywords are in your domain name. Using the above example, if a person types "Tampa Bay Ford" into Google and your domain is tampabayford.com, you have an excellent chance of coming up high on that particular search. Accordingly, make sure to have keywords in your alternate domain names as well.

Tips for Success

No. 1. As already explained, you can own multiple domains. In fact, it's important to do this. Just be certain that they're all redirected to one web site. There's no good reason to have five domain names pointing to five different web sites. This can be costly and confusing to your customers.

No. 2. Don't make your domain name too long. For example, thelongestdomainnameintheworld.com is no fun to type and difficult to remember. Keep the name short and sweet.

No. 3. Try as hard as you can to own the .com for your business name. I also suggest owning .net as well, so no one else can take it.

No. 4. Do a "WHOIS" lookup (a search to see key information about the domain name and its owner) to see when your domain name will expire. You want to make sure that you don't lose the name to someone else by accidentally letting it lapse. See the walkthrough below for directions on how to do a WHOIS lookup.

No. 5. If you find that the domain name you want is taken, you can try to buy it from the owner. To get contact information on the owner, do a WHOIS lookup for that domain name. Sometimes a great domain name is worth a few hundred bucks. But don't overpay for it. If the price is too high, just go back to the drawing board and come up with something better.

No. 6. You should add your name (for example, here's mine: coreyperlman.com) to the list of domain names you want to own. Owning your own name is a worthwhile investment as you never know when you might want to create a web site with your name as the domain.

 Walkthrough: Researching Domain Names

Step 1. Open your browser to mydomain.com, and locate the Search Box toward the top of the page.

Step 2. Enter domain names you're interested in and make sure the .com box is checked. Click the "get my domain" button. Remember, don't add the "www" since it's not needed.

Step 3. Evaluate the results, then answer these two questions:
   A. Is the domain name available? YES or NO
   B. Is the same name ending in .net available? YES or NO

Step 4. Scroll to the bottom of the page.

Step 5. Click on the WHOIS lookup link on the left side of the page. It's way down there, but I promise you'll find it.

Step 6. Think of a domain name that you know is unavailable, such as google.com, then enter it in the blank provided. Click the Search button.

Step 7. Scroll down and evaluate the results.

    A. Who's listed as the registrant for that domain?

    B. What's the email address for the domain owner?

    C. When does the domain name expire?

Once you know who the owner is, you can contact that person to make an offer to buy the domain name. While some names won't be for sale, you'll be surprised at how many will be. If you don't see the contact information for the domain owner, that means they may have paid to keep it private.

Exercise: Buying Domain Names

Now it's time to determine the right domain(s) for your online business. Here's how to proceed.

Step 1. List 10 words that describe your business or that are related to your web site. For example, let's say you own a yoga studio in Tucson, Arizona. Your 10 words might be:

Yoga
Tucson
Arizona
Studio
Meditation
Flexibility
Strength
Practice
Fun
Exercise

Compile your list:
  1.
  2.
  3.
  4.
  5.
  6.
  7.
  8.
  9.
  10.

Step 2. Think of three domains containing some of the above words that might be a good fit for your web site. If you already have a site, come up with three alternative domains. Remember, think of domains that consumers would use when trying to guess what your web site might be. For example:

Choice No. 1: tucsonyoga.com
Choice No. 2: arizonayogastudio.com
Choice No. 3: yogaforfun.com

Now enter your three domains:

Choice No. 1: _____.com
Choice No. 2: _____.com
Choice No. 3: _____.com

Step 3. Open your browser to mydomain.com
Step 4. Enter the domains you listed above in the Search box, then hit the Enter key after each domain in order to move to the next line. Make sure the .com box is checked, and answer these questions:
    A. Is my first choice available?   YES NO
    B. Is my second choice available?   YES NO
    C. Is my third choice available?   YES NO

Step 5. Check the domain(s) you want to own, and click Purchase Domains in the upper-right-hand corner.
Step 6. Create an account by providing the requested information.
Step 7. A two-year contract will now appear on the right side of the screen. If you like, you can decrease the length of the contract or extend it. Now enter your credit card information, and make the purchase.
Step 8. Redirect (or forward) your alternate domains to your main web site. If you have difficulty doing this within mydomain.com, call the technical support line that is provided, and the representative you speak with will gladly assist you.

Case Study

At the beginning of the Internet craze, Ford Motor Company bought all the domains they could think of that related to the name "Ford." The problem, though, was that they didn't think of the names their disgruntled customers had thought of! As a result, embarrassing sites started popping up all over the place, such as fordsucks.com and fordreallysucks.com.

Ford fought back and was able to shut down some of the web sites and take ownership of the domains. Today, if you do a WHOIS lookup for fordsucks.com, you'll see that Ford is the proud owner of this domain name!

The lesson here is not to spend a ton of money, as Ford most likely did, buying up all the domain names that could possibly harm your business. Instead, monitor on a regular basis your most popular searches, such as your name and your web site address. If a negative site ever pops up, you'll know how to contact its owner through a WHOIS lookup, so you can attempt to resolve the conflict and have the negative web site removed.

Resources

mydomain.com is a registrar for buying domain names.
godaddy.com is also a registrar for buying domain names.
icann.org is the governing body for domain names. You can visit its site to view the rules and regulations concerning buying and selling domain names.
internic.net is a subsidiary of icann.org where you can make a claim or initiate a dispute regarding the ownership of a particular domain name.

Cocktail Information

As discussed earlier, country codes are extensions of countries, and the majority can be used only by people living in those countries. Some country codes, however, are available to the public, such as .ca and .tv.

A few years ago, when I worked for the eCommerce Division of General Motors, a group of us inquired about the rights to use the country code .gm. Only the diehard techies would know that this country code belongs to the small African country of Gambia. As this book went to press, .gm was still unavailable for public use. So, unfortunately for General Motors, the domain chevy.gm will just have to wait!

CHAPTER 4

KEYWORDS

The most important list you'll ever make.

In this chapter, you will learn:

The definition of keywords.
Their importance in winning the search engine game.
The exact steps to create the perfect keyword list.
What to avoid when creating your list so you are not
    penalized by the search engines.

Keywords are the words or phrases that people type in the search field when using a search engine. Your goal is to match what they type in the search engine with the words on the front and back end of your web site. I discuss adding keywords to the front end of your web site in the upcoming chapter, Home Page Content. In this chapter, I'll cover how to provide a specific list of keywords that are just meant for the search engines. This list of keywords resides in your source code (behind the scenes) and is not visible on your web site.

Your keyword list should make up all the words that a person would use when looking for your product or service on a search engine. You should include cities in which you do business, product and service names, and other common words used to describe your business. Your keyword list is located in your web page's source code, and usually starts with the header <meta name="Keywords."

As mentioned, the purpose of creating a keyword list is to enable search engines to understand what your web site is about. Without such a list, the engines will default to scanning

Example of a site's keyword list.

```
www.investorteams[1] - Notepad
File  Edit  Format  View  Help

<html>
<head>
<title>Investor Teams. Find Your Team. Find Your Way.</title>
<meta http-equiv="Content-Type" content="text/html; charset=iso-8859-1">
<meta name="keywords" content="investor, investor teams, investor resources, investing, investments, real estate, taxes> stoc
<meta name="description" content="A free site for investors to find educational resources and the right people to make up the
<link href="css.css" rel="stylesheet" type="text/css">
</head>

<body bgcolor="#003366" leftmargin="0" topmargin="0" marginwidth="0" marginheight="0">

<table width="100%" border="0" cellspacing="0" cellpadding="5">
  <tr>
    <td align="center"><table width="768" border="0" cellspacing="0" cellpadding="0">
      <tr>
        <td><table width="100%" border="0" cellspacing="0" cellpadding="0">
          <tr>
            <td><table width="100%" border="0" cellspacing="0" cellpadding="0">
              <tr>
                <td><img src="images/header/leftPanel.jpg" alt="Investor Teams" width="533" height="133"></td>

                <td align="left"><img src="images/header/rtPanel.jpg" width="235" height="133" border="0" usemap="#Map4


              </tr>
            </table></td>
        </tr>
        <tr>
          <td><table width="100%" border="0" cellspacing="0" cellpadding="0">
            <tr>



              <td bgcolor="003366"><img src="images/spacer.gif" width="1" height="10"></td>
```

other parts of your web site to look for keywords. Since this list resides behind the scenes of your web site, you can concentrate solely on the list without it making grammatical or logical sense. For example, people often misspell words when they are searching on Google. You'll want to add those common misspelled words to your keyword list. You may also want to include all the different variations of a particular word. An example might be California, CA, or Cali. You can do this in a keyword list, but it would be inappropriate to include them on your home page content or in other areas visible to someone viewing your web site.

Prioritizing your keyword list is a crucial element to winning the search engine game. The search engines are going to pay most attention to the words or phrases that appear first, so you have to make them good.

Most people make the mistake of beginning their keyword list with names associated with their business. For example, let's say a man named Ray owns a shoe store in Seattle called

Ray's Shoes, the first keyword he might think to list would be "Ray's Shoes." The challenge with this is Ray is not thinking like the majority of the audience he's after. Most people don't know anything about Ray or his business, and they'll go to whichever shoe store they find at the top of their search results.

If I were Ray, I would make my first keyword phrase "Shoe Store Seattle" or "Seattle Shoes" because that's what most people would type in when looking for a shoe store in that city. Of course, Ray still wants to come up high when the name of his business is searched. So the keyword "Ray's Shoes" would certainly make the list. It would just be a lower priority than many of the other more common phrases that people might search for.

The most important thing to do when creating a powerful keyword list is to forget everything you know about your business. Instead, think like a complete stranger who's sitting at his computer early in the morning, sipping a cup of coffee, and just landed on Google. He's about to buy a product you own or use a service you provide. He doesn't care if he buys it from you or from one of your competitors; he just wants to find a business that has what he's looking for and be on his way. What words is he going to type in Google? Answer that question, and you're well on your way to creating a powerful keyword list!

Tips for Success

No. 1. Although some search engines won't accept more than 200 characters in a keyword list, there's no science for how many keywords you should have for every search engine. Some engines will browse your keyword list until they feel they have an understanding of your web site. I feel that a safe range is 15–25 keywords.

No. 2. Keywords can also be key phrases. For example, instead of "house" or "Michigan," use phrases such as "houses in Michigan," "Michigan real estate," and so on.

No. 3. Use common misspelled words as part of your keyword list so you'll attract people who make this frequent error. As an example, General Motors has "Chevrolet" as well as its common misspelling, "Cheverolet," in its keyword list. Smart, huh?

No. 4. Do not repeat keywords. You can use words in phrases more than once but not independently. For example, the right way is "car phone," "car door," and "car window." The wrong way would be "car," "car," and "car."

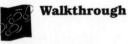 **Walkthrough**

Step 1. Open up Internet Explorer.

Step 2. Go to google.com.

Step 3. Type in the keywords (or phrase) that best describe your business. Remember, think like someone who's looking for your products or services, but has no idea who you are.

Step 4. Click on one of the top three sites that came up on your search.

Step 5. At the top of your browser, find the "View" tab.

Step 6. Then, within the View drop-down, click on "Source."

Step 7. You'll see a page that's full of nonsense and looks like hieroglyphics.

However, see if you can locate the words "<meta keywords=" toward the top of the page. If you don't see these words, go to another site and repeat these steps.

Step 8. Evaluate this web site's keyword list. Since a web site's keywords are in the public domain, don't be bashful about evaluating a competitor's keyword list to help you develop yours. I didn't say copy their list, but just look for ways to make your keyword list stronger.

Exercise

Author's note: This exercise is very important and requires a good deal of time and attention. I recommend that you spend an entire afternoon or evening on it, and include others (spouse, colleague, friend) in the brainstorming process. Keep an open mind and have fun with the process. On Friday nights, my wife and I will often invite other couples over, open a few bottles of wine, and exchange keyword ideas. A good ol' fashioned nerds night out!

Step 1. Start thinking about your business, the services or products you provide, and how you help people.

Step 2. Write down 30 words or phrases that describe your business:

_____

_____

_____

_____

_____

_____

Step 3. Write down the 30 words or phrases that your spouse, colleagues, and friends chose to describe your business:

_____

_____

_____

_____

_____

_____

Step 4. Now close your eyes and put yourself in the shoes of a potential customer who has no idea who you are or what you do. All this person knows is that he or she needs a service or product that your web site provides. Remember, you are now in the mind of a potential customer. Write down the first 10 phrases that come to mind:

_____

_____

_____

_____

_____

_____

Step 5. Take the three lists and prioritize them into one list of 20 words or phrases. Remember to localize your list by including cities and counties you do business in.

_____

_____

_____

_____

_____

_____

Congratulations! You have just created your keywords for your web site.

Case Study

Last year, I was asked to conduct a workshop for a group of Shaklee Independent Distributors. Shaklee Independent Distributors market environmentally safe cleaning products and natural nutritional supplements using a Social Marketing™ business model. This was an unusual crowd for me because I had about 12 business owners in a room and they all sold the exact same products.

When it came time for the exercise where we created a keyword list, I was concerned that each person's list would be the same, again, since they all sold the same line of products. I was pleasantly surprised that each person had a completely different set of keywords that they had created. This was because each person had carved out a specific niche within their business that they wanted to focus on. One person was an expert on diet and fitness and wanted to attract customers looking to lose weight and become healthier. Another was a mother of young children and wanted to make sure the cleaning products she used in her home were safe for her kids and wanted to help others do the same.

So even though all 12 people had the same line of products to sell, each came up with a specific person they wanted to attract to their web site and therefore came up with a unique list of keyword phrases.

The workshop ended up being a win-win for everyone. They each created a great list of keywords, and I left with a basket of safe cleaning products and some great-tasting breakfast shakes!

Resources

http://marketing.networksolutions.com/web-promotion-tools.php is a keyword suggestion tool. wordtracker.com is one of the most popular keyword suggestion tools.

https://adwords.Google.com/select/KeywordToolExternal is Google's keyword suggestion tool.

CHAPTER 5

TITLE TAG

*A search engine's first impression
of your web site—make it a good one.*

In this chapter, you will learn:

The definition of a title tag.
Its importance in winning the search engine game.
The exact steps to create the perfect title tag.

A title tag is the headline of a web site. It appears at the top of your browser on every web page you visit. If you use Internet Explorer, it resides at the very top of your page in the blue bar with the "e" in the upper right-hand corner. And I bet you've never even noticed it before. Well, that's about to change as you will soon learn how important that one little sentence is in winning the search engine game.

One of the biggest misconceptions about Google and other search engines is that *they* decide how your web site appears on their search engine. On the contrary! Google and other search engines have nothing to do with it. They control where you're *placed*, but you control how your web site link and its subsequent content *appear* on their search engine.

When the search engines evaluate your web site, they use your title tag as the blue link that appears when they list your site. They simply take the headline from your web site (way up there in the blue bar) and place it directly in their engine as the link to your web site. Your title tag makes up half of the entire real estate you are given on Google and the other search engines. (You'll learn about the other half in the next chapter.) This is why

The title tag is located in the blue bar at the top of your browser.

From your site to Google's!

it's so important for you to create the perfect title tag for your business. It's the first of two sentences that will ultimately determine if a searcher clicks on your link or on a competitor's.

As mentioned above, your title tag contains the first words someone sees when your web site comes up on a search engine, so you have to make it STAND OUT over all the rest. The goal of your title tag is to make everyone crystal clear as to who you are and what you do.

As important as title tags are, time and time again you'll notice web sites that just list the web site name as its title tag or simply use the default text "home page," as seen in the example below. And worse yet, if no title tag exists, "untitled document" is all that will appear as the blue link in Google. To see an example of this, simply search for "untitled document" in Google and you'll find thousands of web sites with this issue.

Here's an example
of a default title tag.

Even if your web site has a title tag, you want it to be more than just the name of your web site or your business. You are given space for about ten words in most search engines for your title tag. Use that precious space to create a powerful headline for your business.

Your title tag is also a great place to incorporate keywords. You should try to include some of your best words as it's one of the first places search engines look when evaluating a web site.

Now it's time to create the perfect title tag, one that will stand out as the headline to your web site. Make sure to include plenty of keywords, and feel free to be creative so yours stands head and shoulders above the rest.

Tips for Success

No. 1. Make sure your title tag is between five and 10 words in length.

No. 2. Each page within your web site has the opportunity to appear in a search engine, and therefore should have its own title tag. The title tag should explain that particular page. For example, if you have a web site that sells printers, the purchase page could have a title tag that reads "Purchase Page for Steve's Printers in Denver, Colorado."

No. 3. Include important keywords in the title tags for each of the web pages on your site.

No. 4. Google and other search engines only give enough space for about eight words in your title tag before they cut the sentence off. If you go over the allotted space, the excess words won't be visible to the user. So make those few words count!

No. 5. Put your keyword-heavy headline in front of the name of your business in your title tag. Google and other search engines put more weight on the first words of your title tag, so you want to have those keywords before the name of your business.

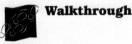 **Walkthrough**

Step 1. Open Internet Explorer.

Step 2. Go to google.com.

Step 3. Type "paint it yourself pottery Michigan" in the search box.

Step 4. Locate the first search result, and write down the words highlighted in blue:

These words are the site's title tag.

Step 5. Click on the link of the web site's title tag that you listed above.

Step 6. Look at the blue bar at the very top of your browser where the Internet Explorer logo is an "e."

Step 7. Write down the words that follow the "e":

_____

Step 8. Click on the "View" tab at the top of the page and click "View Source" from the drop-down.

Step 9. Locate the <title> tag close to the top and write it below:

_____

You should have written down the same sentence each time. Your title tag is found in the source code of your web site as well as at the top of your browser. Search engines take this title tag and use it as the blue, highlighted link in their search results. That's why it's essential to have a clear, concise title tag that grabs the attention of searchers and makes them want to click on your web site.

 Exercise: Create Your Title Tag

Step 1. Create your title tag, and remember to keep it between 5–8 words long. Try to include as many keywords as you can.

_____

_____

Case Study

I recently got married in Boca Grande, Florida, and there was a wonderful steel drummer who performed during the cocktail hour. In one of our conversations, I mentioned to him that I help small business owners with their Internet marketing. He asked if I would take a look at his web site and provide some recommendations. His issue was not his presence on the search engines, since his web site usually does quite well with most of his popular keyword searches. His problem was that people were not clicking on his web site when they came across his search result. That's because his title tag read "Pan Paradise – Home Page" (See image above).

I explained to him that when people search for a steel drum band, they have no idea what Pan Paradise means and therefore skip over his web site when it appears in their search results. He quickly changed his title tag to "Steel drummer and steel drum band in Keys, Miami, Ft. Lauderdale, Naples, West Palm Beach and other Florida cities." Now, not only is his site coming up high on the search engines, but he's getting that traffic to click on his web site.

Here is his new title tag!

Resources

http://videos.webpronews.com/2006/10/18/title-tag-tips/
provides videos and article with title-tag tips.
http://pdxtc.com/seo101/scotts-articles/organic-search/
title-tag-tips.html discusses five rules for creating a title tag.

META DESCRIPTION TAG

Your chance to tell a search engine user why they should click on your link over all the others.

The definition of a meta description tag.
Its importance in winning the search engine game.
How to use it in conjunction with your title tag.
The exact steps to create the perfect meta description tag.

Your title tag is the headline of your web site, and your meta description tag is the sub-headline. It's more descriptive and longer than the title tag. If you look at the search engine below, the meta description tag is the black text directly under the blue highlighted link.

Both your title tag and description tag are the only two gateways between a search engine and your web site. Your meta description tag should complement your title tag by providing a more detailed description of what your web site is about. Between the two, there should be no doubt as to who you are and exactly what products or services you provide. And most importantly, your meta description tag should sell the searcher on why they should go to your web site over all the others.

Unfortunately, most business owners leave the creation of their title tag and meta description tag to their web designer. As you can now see, the only one who should be creating these two critical sentences is you, the business owner.

Before creating your meta description tag, let's go over a few guidelines for writing one. Similar to your title tag, the description tag should be written as a sentence or phrase, but it should be longer and more descriptive than the title tag. There's also a character or word limit as to how long your description tag can be. Because all search engines have different maximum word counts, I recommend that your description tag be 20–25 words long. After about 25 words, search engines will just cut off the tag, as shown in the example below.

As with your keywords and title tag, search engines can find your meta description tag in the source code of your web site.

Below is an opportunity to create that perfect meta description tag to go along with your title tag and the list of keywords that you created in Chapter 4. Once complete, you'll send this list off to your Web designer to be immediately added to the back end of your web site.

Tips for Success

No. 1. Make sure your description tag is extremely descriptive and clearly explains what your web site does.

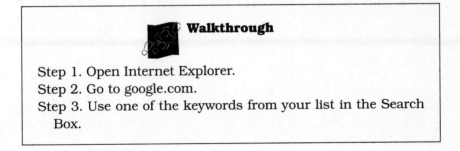

No. 2. Use keywords in your description tag because search engines like to review them when evaluating a site.

No. 3. Be sure to do a little selling in your description tag. You have only two sentences (your title tag and description tag) to persuade a person to click on your site instead of all the others.

No. 4. If you need ideas on what to write, look at other web site's description tags by going to their site, clicking on "View" and then "Source." You can also just do a Google search and review the black text under the blue link.

Walkthrough

Step 1. Open Internet Explorer.
Step 2. Go to google.com.
Step 3. Use one of the keywords from your list in the Search Box.

Step 4. Locate the title tag of one of the top three search results. (Remember, the title tag is the blue, highlighted text.)

Step 5. Locate the meta description tag, which is the black text underneath the title tag (see images above).

Step 6. Review a few of the meta description tags you see on the page, and write down what you like and dislike about them.

_____

_____

_____

_____

_____

Hopefully, you'll start to notice the web sites where people spent time creating their meta description tags as well as the sites where the sentence was simply pulled from the web site's home page content. Once you've looked at and evaluated other description tags, it's time to create your own!

 Exercise

Step 1. Create your 20 to 25-word meta description tag. Remember, it should be more descriptive than your title tag, and make sure to include keywords that your potential customers might use to find you. Also, be certain that it explains what your site does and why you're the best in the business!

_____

_____

_____

_____

Step 2. Paste your description tag, along with your title tag and keywords, in an e-mail, and send it to your web designer. As a guide, I've typed this e-mail message:

Dear <insert web designer's name>,

Please upload the meta tags listed below to my web site. You'll find a list of keywords along with my title tag and meta description tag.

Thanks so much,

<insert your name here>

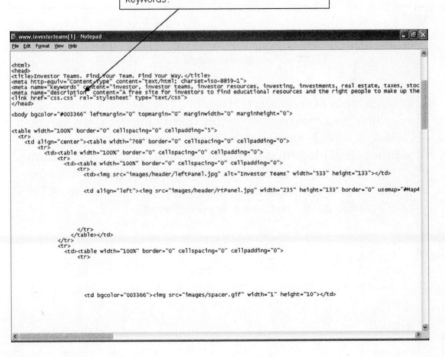

The description tag is located in your source code, usually below the title tag and keywords.

Bonus Exercise (To be completed after your meta tags have been added to your web site)

Step 1. Open your browser and go to monsterwebpromotion. com. You'll notice it's a Network Solutions web site.

Step 2. Click on "Tools."

Step 3. Scroll to the bottom of the page and enter your web site in the space below the header: Search Engine Spider Simulator.

Step 4. Click submit.

The results you see are exactly what the search engines see when they arrive at your site. You should see your homepage content, keywords, title tag, meta description tag, and so on. If you don't see any of your meta tags or are concerned about any content that you do see, contact your web designer for assistance.

Resources

highrankings.com/metadescription.htm is an article on creating a meta description tag.

searchengines.com/metadescription.html provides tips for creating a search-engine-friendly meta description tag.

seomoz.org/blog/making-the-most-of-meta-description-tags is a blog (an online journal that you can create, also the subject of Chapter 11) posting on how to maximize the effectiveness of your meta description tag.

Cocktail Information

I recently visited one of Google's offices in New York City. As I toured the exciting facility, I spoke with some of the employees about the Internet marketing boot camps I teach, specifically how I teach people to create their own meta tags so they can take control of how their web site appears in search engines such as Google. In unison, they all thanked me for spreading that message to the public. They told me that one of the most common calls they receive is from frantic Google users upset about how their web site is showing up on Google's search engine. With the calls following in rapid succession, Google employees must take time explaining to each one how they don't control how the search results appear on the page, but that the web site owner actually has full control. One of the employees then patted me on the back and said he hopes my message gets out to the masses soon so he can finally get some work done!

CHAPTER 7

HOME PAGE CONTENT

This critical content must be created with two audiences in mind: your customers and the search engines.

In this chapter, you will learn:

How your home page content influences the search engines.
How to make your content friendly to both your customers
  and the search engines.
Tips for creating content that will help you avoid penalties
  from search engines.

Along with evaluating your keywords, title tag, and meta
description tag, search engines will also search for keywords
within the content of your web site when determining where you
should rank on their site. Although search engines will evaluate
all of the pages within your web site, this chapter will focus on
your homepage because that's usually where the search engines
will begin evaluating your site.

When talking about home page content, I'm talking about the
written words found on the main page of your web site. When
search engines evaluate a home page, they look for words that frequently appear in the content of the page. To win the search engine
game, you need to incorporate keywords into the content of your
home page. Later in this chapter, you'll have the opportunity to evaluate your current home page content and look for ways to make it
more keyword friendly.

Even though adding keywords to your home page can help
you win the search engine game, you can't write your home page
content solely for the search engine audience. You have a much-
too-important audience to focus on: *your web site visitors!* So you
must make your primary objective creating powerful, easy-to-read

content that perfectly delivers your message to your readers. Be creative and find ways to incorporate your most important keywords while sticking to your primary objective.

There are multiple areas on your home page where you can include keywords. The primary area, of course, is the main content of your web site. Here, you should have a paragraph or two that describes what your site is about and how you help your customers. This is the area where you should spend most of your time, adding keywords wherever appropriate.

You can also add keywords to the links on your site. Make sure to use words as your links, not graphics, so the search engines can easily read them. For example, if you have a page in your site to sell workout equipment, it's better to have a link that says "workout equipment" than an image of dumbbells or a weight bench.

Also, be careful about using too much animation, like video or graphics with motion, on your home page. These types of web sites are great to look at, but they can wreak havoc on your search-engine ranking because there is no content for them to evaluate.

Make sure your web designer understands that you want your web site to be search engine friendly, and that this is a priority when designing your site.

Tips for Success

No. 1. Although it's important to use keywords multiple times throughout your site, be careful not to overdo it. You don't want to repeat these words over and over. This is called "keyword stuffing," and search engines can omit you from their search results if they believe you're guilty of doing this. Just be certain that the sentence makes grammatical sense and is logical to your readers. If you accomplish this, you shouldn't have anything to worry about.

Here's an example of keyword stuffing: "We sell art in many states throughout the U.S., including Nevada art, Ohio art, Pennsylvania art, Kentucky art, and so on."

And here's the sentence prepared properly: "We sell art in many states throughout the U.S., including Nevada, Ohio, Pennsylvania, Kentucky, and so on."

No. 2. Keep the ratio between a keyword and the total number of words on your home page between four percent and 10 percent. To figure out the ratio of a particular keyword, divide the number of times you use that word by how many words appear on your home page. In the exercise below, there's a convenient tool that will do the math for you.

No. 3. This may appear to be obvious, but it's worth stating: Always spell-check your web site content, and ask others to proofread it. There's nothing that can kill your credibility quicker than a blatant spelling error on your home page.

 Walkthrough

Step 1. Go to webconfs.com and click on "Keyword Density Checker."

Step 2. Enter your web site into the Keyword Density Analyzer and hit "submit."

You will see a keyword cloud where the most common words on your home page are indicated by the size of the word. You can also see an exact count of each word below the keyword cloud.

Write down the most frequently used words on your home page:

_____

Now record the important keywords that are not at the top of your list:

_____

Step 3. If filler words, such as "a," "and," "the," and "or" are at the top of your list, you need to make some adjustments to increase the frequency of your most important keywords.

Exercise: Create Your Home Page Content

Step 1. Go to your web site and evaluate the content on your homepage.

Step 2. Using the above information, rewrite the opening paragraph of your home page. Remember, you're writing for two audiences: your customers and the search engines.

_____

_____

_____

_____

_____

_____

Step 3. Continue to evaluate the rest of the content on your homepage and make changes where necessary.

Step 4. Send your new homepage content to your web designer and ask him or her to upload it to your web site.

Case Study

Here's an experience that's dear to my heart.

My father wrote a book called *The Nurturing Father's Program* to help dads become better fathers. Now, my dad is an excellent writer, a great speaker, and a pretty good father himself. But the Internet was an unfamiliar and scary place for him, and he desperately needed some search-engine exposure for his web site.

I sat down with him one night and evaluated his situation. He had a great domain, good meta tags, and multiple web sites had his link on their sites. I couldn't figure out what the problem was. Then I checked out his home page. He had plenty of writing on the site, but he had not taken into account the importance of making his home page content search engine friendly.

I deleted the entire content from his home page. After a brief screaming session, followed by a walk around the block so we both could cool off, we rewrote the home page from scratch. The new content consisted of frequently used words, such as "fathering," "nurturing," "parenting," and "program."

I still didn't have my dad convinced that spending the entire night rewriting his content would make any difference to the search engines. That was until two weeks later when we googled "nurturing fathers," and his web site was the first to appear. The smile on his face was priceless and all the thanks I needed. I said, "Pops, you taught me how to drive, ride my bike, play basketball . . . we're even, right?" He quickly replied, "Let's not go overboard."

Web Tidbit

I wrote an article on the five things your web designer might have missed when designing your home page. For your free copy, go to ebootcampbook.com/freearticle.

Resources

www.webconfs.com provides a free tool for calculating the frequency of each word on your home page.

http://marketing.networksolutions.com/web-promotion-tools.php is an alternative free tool for calculating the frequency of each word on your home page.

http://searchenginewatch.com/showPage.html?page=2168021 contains an article discussing the importance of placing keywords on your home page.

CHAPTER 8

LINK POPULARITY

Learn how to increase your web site's popularity and become more noticeable with the search engines.

Remember back in high school when you could be popular one minute, but then the next minute be sitting home alone on prom night? And your teenage crush, let's call her Jennifer Dellanbach, didn't even call that night because she was going to the prom with one Steven Anderson, whom she knew you hated. *Why Jennifer, why?* Um, sorry . . . where was I?

Ah, yes, I was about to make the point that just as being popular in high school will get you to the prom and the best parties, being popular on the Internet will help you win the search engine game.

Link popularity, by definition, is a tool that search engines use to measure the quantity and quality of web sites that link to your site. Search engines feel that if your web site is mentioned on other sites, that gives it credibility and therefore should reflect positively on your ranking. This is the foundation of how Google determines where to rank web sites on their search engine.

So the first thought that should be going through your head is how many web sites currently have a link to your site. Using linkpopularity.com (see the walkthrough below), you can do an analysis of the largest search engines to see what web sites they find that link back to your web site. Could there be more out there that the search engines just didn't pick up? Yes, but they don't matter because you only get credit from the search engine if they can find it. So take these results very seriously.

You might be pleasantly surprised to find web sites on the list that you've never heard of before and have no idea how or why they decided to link to you. Generally you can just chalk that up to good karma and leave them alone. They are working positively for your web site's search engine rankings. The only exception to that is if you explore the site and find that it either misrepresents you or has subject matter that you don't agree with.

But more often than not, you'll find the number is probably low or possibly even zero. Hey, don't beat yourself up; the rest of this chapter is dedicated to helping you boost your link popularity, and you can use linkpopularity.com to monitor your progress. If you are like me, you'll start checking your link popularity like you do your stocks or your favorite sports scores. And you will have passed yet another test toward your official nerd certification training.

So let's get the wrong way to approach link popularity out of the way first. Many years ago, when web site designers and SEO companies caught wind of how search engines operate, they started adding their clients' web site link to as many other sites as they could. Some even went so far as to create web sites for the sole purpose of adding a client's link to them. The only content on these sites would be web site links, and they came to be known as "link farms." Link farms are now frowned upon by the search engines because they aren't real indicators of popularity. It's like paying people to come to your party. So don't use link farms to increase your link popularity.

Another approach that I would shy away from is having your link displayed on any web site, irrespective of its content. It's not just about quantity, but quality. Search engines will look for how relevant a web site is to your business. For example, let's say you own a tile company. A search engine will give you more credit for your link to be on a homebuilder's web site than on someone's travel web site. So to give yourself the best chance of being deemed popular by the search engines, you'll want to have your link on multiple web sites that are real sites and have some sort of relevancy to your business.

You now know the mission at hand: approach other web sites to add a link back to your web site. Use the rest of this chapter to create a list of web sites that you will contact and ask to add your link to their site. Soon you will become Mr. or Mrs. Popular, and together we can show the Jennifer Dellanbachs of the world what they missed out on!

Tips for Success

No. 1. There are multiple ways to have your link added to a web site. For example, you can write an article to be used as content for a web site, and then place your link at the end of it. You can also offer a testimonial to a web site whose product or service you've used, with, of course, a link to your web site included at the end of it.

No. 2. Use the art of reciprocity. If you have links on your web site to other sites, those sites should be more than willing to return the favor and add your link to their web site.

No. 3. The Chamber of Commerce is a great resource when looking for web sites to add your link to.

No. 4. The popularity of the web sites that link to you is also important. If you know of some web sites that receive a lot of traffic, make those a priority!

No. 5. Every vendor that you pay money to should have no problem adding a link back to your site. Just ask!

 Walkthrough

Step 1. Open your browser to linkpopularity.com.

Step 2. Enter your web site address in the box provided, and click on "Tell me my popularity."

Step 3. Click on one of the search engines listed and evaluate your results.

Author's Note: You can also check your link popularity directly in Google by typing the following information into Google's search field: link:www.yourdomain.com. So if you wanted to check the popularity of my favorite coffee shop, you'd type link:www.cariboucoffee.com into Google's search box.

Exercise

Step 1. List five web sites that you'll approach to have your link added to their site:

_____

_____

_____

_____

_____

Step 2. E-mail or call the owner of each web site, and ask if they would be agreeable to adding your link to one of the pages in their site. Remember to offer a space on your site for their web site. They will be much more open to a two-way street than just saying yes to your request.

Case Study

A company, we'll call it ABC Corporation to maintain confidentiality, hired a search engine optimization (SEO) company to optimize its web site. The SEO promised to increase ABC's link popularity, and for all intents and purposes they were sincere about what they promised. What the SEO failed to mention, however, is exactly which web sites they were going to add ABC's link to. They chose link farm sites, which, as just discussed, are web sites whose sole purpose is to house links to other sites. This is a tactic frowned upon by most search engine companies, and, as a result, ABC did not see much improvement in its traffic or search engine ranking.

When I was brought in as a consultant for ABC, I did a link popularity check on linkpopularity.com, and I immediately discovered what the issue was. I informed ABC that search engines are constantly improving their search formulas and have recently been able to distinguish between link farm sites and actual relevant web sites. I also explained that an additional benefit to having their link on other relevant web sites is the possibility that people will click on the link and visit their site. By placing ABC's link on company sites they do business with, it would give them a much greater chance of receiving more traffic to their site from these sources.

Armed with this information, I quickly took ABC off the link farm sites and added their link to partnership companies, vendors, local government sites and so on. ABC quickly achieved a positive impact on its search engine rankings as well as increased traffic to its web site.

Resources

linkpopularity.com is a free service that will test your link popularity by listing all the web sites in Google, Yahoo, and MSN that have a link to your web site.

selfseo.com/story-19601.php offers an article about the importance of link popularity when being ranked by Google.

netmechanic.com/news/vol6/promo_no5.htm provides 10 ways to increase your link popularity.

Example of linkpopularity.com

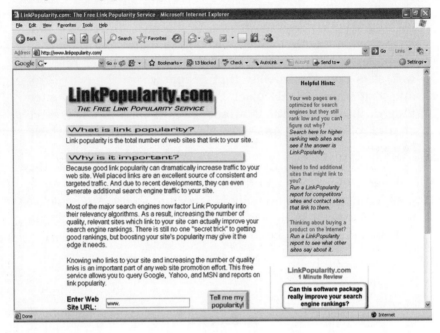

Cocktail Information

In 1995, a graduate of Stanford University named Larry Page created a formula for ranking web pages based on their popularity. He coined the formula "PageRank," and continued to tweak the formula for the next two or three years. With the help of a partner, Sergey Brin, Page's formula became a functional prototype that, in 1998, they named "Google." This became the foundation for Google, Inc., and PageRank is still one of the factors that Google uses to analyze search results.

CREATE A WEB PRESENCE TO DOMINATE THE SEARCH ENGINES AND DRASTICALLY INCREASE TRAFFIC TO YOUR WEB SITE

INTRODUCTION

Gone are the days of using your web site as your sole Internet marketing tool. Instead, small businesses are creating what's known as a "web presence" to funnel people into their web site from all different directions. A web presence is a group of online resources that can individually drive traffic to your web site. Some of these resources include networking sites like myspace.com as well as blogs, press releases, and e-newsletters (an electronic magazine or newsletter).

Here's how it works. Picture a spider web with your web site in the middle of it. Your objective is to attract as many people to the spider's web as possible. Each time you create a different resource, like a blog or enewsletter, you're expanding your web. And by including a link from each of your resources directly to your web site, you're funneling all traffic directly to the center of your site, as seen in the picture below.

Funneling traffic to your web site is only the beginning. You will also want to direct your customers to other parts of your web presence. You might refer to your blog in your MySpace page or ask people to sign up for your monthly e-newsletter from inside your blog. The point is to keep people engaged with your valuable content. This will help you build credibility with your readers and create lifelong customers!

Besides the advantage of creating more opportunities for people to find you, creating a web presence is also an extremely

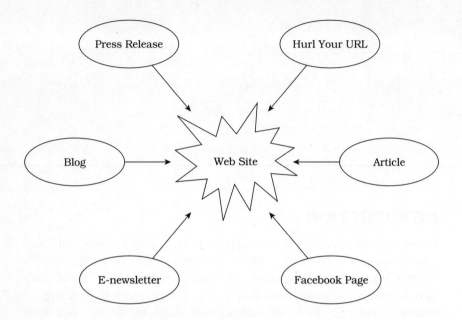

powerful tool for winning the search engine game. Many of the resources you create, such as a blog, press release, or article, are actually web pages themselves, and each can compete for search engine placement. It's no longer uncommon to do a search on google.com and find many of the results to be blogs, press releases, or videos, sometimes all created by the same person or business.

When you have a web presence, you're not just competing to come up first on a search engine. Instead, you're looking to dominate all 10 results with content about your business. Not only is your content moving up the search engine rankings, but you're also squeezing competitors out of those precious top 10 search results.

A large part of having a web presence is delivering content about your subject matter that your users will find valuable. No matter what business you're in, you have information that's worth its weight in gold to the general public. Take dentists, for example. Their knowledge on how to keep teeth white or the safest way to floss is information that might be common knowledge to them,

Here is how the ultimate web presence should look like:

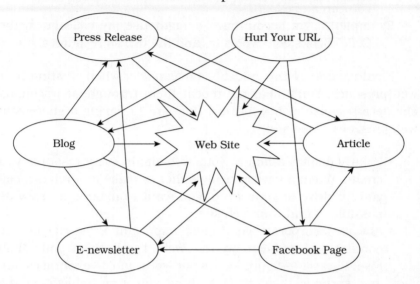

but invaluable advice to others. If my dentist decided to put those types of tips in an e-mail that he sent to me monthly, I promise you it would be one of the first that I'd open. I'd even forward it on to some of my "floss only on even years" friends out there!

The content you use for the different resources can be created by you, republished from something you once wrote, or borrowed from some other source. Of course, if you borrow content, you must cite the author and where it came from. Here are some questions to get you thinking about the valuable content you have to offer:

What's your expertise?

Example: I'm an accountant, and I'm very familiar with the different corporate entities, 1031 exchanges, QuickBooks, and so on.

Think of three topics that you could write about that would interest your customers.

Example: As an accountant, I could write about the differences between an S-corp and a C-corp, the advantages of doing a 1031 exchange, and five tips for making QuickBooks a breeze.

Think of three sources that provide excellent content about
your area of expertise.

Example: As an accountant, I might use my colleagues, the
QuickBooks.com web site, and the IRS as resources.

Finally, here are five guidelines to consider when creating your
web presence. You'll hear me repeat them throughout upcoming
chapters because of how critical they are to having a successful
web presence. They are:

- Clearly display a link to your web site in every resource you
  create. When a user is ready either to make a purchase, call
  you, or drive to your store, you want to make it as easy as
  possible to find your web site.
- Always incorporate your most important keywords in any
  content you publish on the Web. I call them your "Fab
  Five Phrases"—figure out what your fab five phrases are
  and sprinkle them in everything you ever publish on the
  Internet.
- Try to keep your branding consistent throughout your web
  presence. If the colors of your web site are purple and gold,
  use these colors in your blog, e-newsletter, and so on.
- Republish, republish, republish! If you write a great article,
  you can use it in your blog, e-newsletter, web site, and more!
- Add value first, sell second. When you have a web presence,
  you're creating relationships with your customers. If you
  sell your products or services too hard, you'll lose readers.
  Provide great value in your web presence, and you'll keep
  your customers engaged. Then, when you do have something to promote or sell, they'll be more likely to be open to
  your marketing message.

When you've completed this section, you'll have all the tools
you need to create these powerful resources and start building
your web presence. So take a sip of your favorite beverage, and
get that pencil ready. It's time to go to work.

CHAPTER 9

HURL YOUR URL

The easiest way to effectively market your web site.

In this chapter, you will learn:

Why it is important to Hurl Your Url.
Cost-effective ways to Hurl Your Url.
Things to remember when Hurling Your Url.

Before we get started, I'd like you to stop reading for a moment and go get your business card. Did your web site address make it on the card? If the answer is yes, give yourself a pat on the back. If not, smack yourself around a little and have new cards printed up ASAP. Your business card should always include your web site address!

Your business card is just one example of an easy way to advertise your web site address or to "Hurl Your URL" (URL stands for Uniform Resource Locator, which is a techie term for your web site).

Hurl Your URL is just a catchy, easy-to-remember phrase that will serve as a constant reminder to advertise your web site in everything you do. Here are some ideas.

Do you have a car? This is a mobile billboard great for advertising your web site address.

How about marketing materials like flyers and a letterhead? Make sure to add your web site address to them.

Further possibilities include offering coupons containing your web address or, for example, sponsoring your kid's soccer team, with your URL on their jerseys.

Does your teenager keep nagging you for a tattoo? If the answer is yes, I've got the perfect win-win situation for the two of you. You allow your son or daughter to get the tattoo they've been begging for under one condition: the tattoo must display the name of your web site address. They get to desecrate their body and you get to Hurl Your URL!

In all seriousness, expanding the visibility of your URL is the most underutilized, as well as cost-effective, way to promote your web site. All you need to do is to be creative. No matter where you're walking, running, biking, driving, or eating, be on the look-out for new ways to market your business. The possibilities are endless.

Tips for Success

No. 1. Be sure you've finalized your domain name (see chapter 3) before you start an aggressive marketing campaign targeted to the public. The last thing you want is a thousand flyers or business cards that list your old web site address.

No. 2. If you're having difficulty fitting your web site address onto your business card, consider shortening the name.

No. 3. I know from personal experience that offline advertising can be expensive. Try to find organizations or not-for-profit groups that you can donate your time or products to. Often, they'll allow you to advertise your business at their events. You'll be doing a great service to people in need, and you'll also be Hurling Your URL!

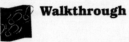 **Walkthrough**

Step 1. Take a walk around your office building or through your home and look for items with a web site address on them. Look for coffee mugs, pencils, magnets—anything you can find.

Step 2. List the first five you found:

_____

_____

_____

_____

Step 3. If you found any items that would serve as a great marketing promotion, use them in the exercise below.

Exercise

Step 1. List five offline resources for adding your web site address to:

1. _____

2. _____

3. _____

4. _____

5. _____

Step 2. Commit to a date and time when you'll add your web site to at least one of the items above.

Case Study

My wife, Jessica, owns a pottery store in the lovely town of Plymouth, Michigan. She's a small business owner and also a graduate of my Internet marketing course. Is that how we met? You'll have to wait until until the sequel: eBoot Camp—A Romance Novel.

During a recent seminar, I wanted to award the participants with prizes after they answered questions correctly. So I asked Jessica if she would make some coffee mugs with my web site address on them to use as giveaways. She said sure and proceeded to make 15 great-looking mugs.

When she gave the mugs to me, I immediately saw that my web site was neatly placed on the outside of each one, just like I had asked. To my surprise, I noticed that Jessica's web site appeared on the inside of every mug. "Always looking for opportunities to Hurl my URL!" she said. Once the student, now the teacher!

Resources

sgotek.com is a direct mail company that can give you enormous distribution for printed materials that contain your web site.

vistaprint.com prints postcards, if you think this marketing method would be effective.

webdecal.com can place your web site on your car.

cafepress.com produces T-shirts, mugs, and so on, that can display your web site.

Web Tidbit

Here's a great way to Hurl Your URL and put a smile on this author's face at the same time! Have you enjoyed this book so far? You can go to ebootcamprocks.com and submit a testimonial. Make sure to include your URL, and if I post your testimonial on my web site or future books, I'll make sure to Hurl Your URL for you!

CHAPTER 10

SOCIAL NETWORKING SITES

Find new business quickly and effectively and do it in your pajamas if you'd like.

In this chapter, you will learn:

Why social networking sites are a great way to grow your
  business.
The three sites that I recommend using.
How to maximize their effectiveness.
How social networking sites impact your search engine
  ranking.

Social networking sites are web sites where people can communicate with each other online. These sites are largely used to
find and connect with past and current friends. But many people
are realizing these sites are also a very powerful networking tool
to find new customers and share information about their products and services.

The two largest social networking sites are facebook.com
and myspace.com. Now be honest, raise your hand if you think
Facebook and MySpace are basically high school and college
hangouts in cyberspace. I'll bet the chances are good that your
hand is up, and so was mine not too long ago. That was the case
until I found out that almost half of the Facebook and MySpace
users are older than 35. In fact, a 2007 ComScore report showed
that 40 percent of Facebook users are older than 35 and over
50 percent are older than 25. And this web site still signs up an
astonishing 230,000 people every day!

So what does this all mean? Both Facebook and MySpace have become free and easy ways to connect with people and foster business relationships.

So if you are still not sure if Facebook and MySpace are your cups of tea, I've got a third option that is perfect for a more mature audience. LinkedIn.com has a much smaller audience (approximately 10 million as this book goes to press), but the sole focus of this site is business networking as it does not promote itself to the teenage or college audience. LinkedIn is easy to use and has some great features for marketing your business. Since I enjoy the benefits of all of these networking resources, I'm going to recommend that you create a page on each of them. But, if you want to start with just one, go with LinkedIn as your primary social networking site.

The process to start social networking is easy and extremely cost-effective. As with most of my recommendations, the only cost is a few hours of your time. The first step is to go to one of the web sites I've recommended and sign-up for a free account. You will then fill out a bio about your business. Once complete, you will start to search for people on the site with like-minded interests and request to make a connection with them. If they accept, they become part of your network. Rinse and repeat at the other two sites that I listed above. A step-by-step process for setting up your page is outlined in the exercise section below.

If you're wondering why a busy guy or gal like you should spend valuable time networking on these sites, it's because they're so effective. With these sites, you can create a network of contacts that dwarfs the number of relationships you can form at a face-to-face networking event. You can do your networking late at night or on the weekends, at your favorite coffee shop or in the comfort of your home. You can also target your audience with pinpoint accuracy by using the search capabilities these online networking sites offer. For example, search for "robotic equipment buyers in Dallas, Texas," and you'll view hundreds of people who are engaged in that type of activity.

By creating a page on each of these sites, you can build relationships with people by inviting them to become part of your network. Once you've made the connection, you can begin communicating with them and learn more about their business and how you might be able to help them. The opportunities are endless. And the cost is just time, and not a lot of it. Simply follow the steps below, and you'll have the majority of the work completed.

Example of a linkedin.com page.

Tips for Success

No. 1. On most networking sites, you'll be allowed to accept or deny connections from other people. Try to accept only people from trusted sources. If you're unsure (especially when using MySpace), lean on the side of caution, and don't accept the request or ask for more details as to why they're interested in connecting with you. Unfortunately, the spammers (people who make connections with you just to sell you products) have caught on to the networking trend, and would love to add you to their list.

No. 2. Be professional. One of the neatest features of networking sites is the ability to find old friends and former flames. But the last thing you need is a bunch of people posting funny comments on your site about old times. Feel free to create a personal page for these connections, but leave the business page strictly to business contacts.

No. 3. Use all the features that Facebook, MySpace, or LinkedIn offer. Post pictures of your business operations in action, or add video of customer testimonials.

No. 4. Most important, make sure your web site link is prominently displayed on all your networking sites. Always Hurl Your URL!

Exercise

Here, you'll create a template for all of your social networking pages. Once you complete this exercise, copy it to the sites that you decide to join. You'll have most of the upfront work done and will be able to focus on building your network.

Step 1. Name of your company:

_____

Step 2. Company objectives:

_____
_____
_____

Step 3. Industries with which your company is associated:

_____
_____
_____

Step 4. Advertisement about an upcoming event, product launch, and so on:

_____
_____
_____

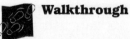 **Walkthrough**

Here's how to create a page on linkedin.com.

Step 1. Open your browser to linkedin.com, and register for a free account.

Step 2. Answer the series of questions so LinkedIn can help you start your network.

Step 3. Start inviting people to become part of your network. If your business is real estate, for example, you can search for real estate agents, mortgage brokers, or even people who have real estate as an interest.

You can be very selective as to the people you invite into your network, and the more selective you are the better the chances that those people will accept your request. Understand that some will say no, but don't be offended. The more people you invite, the greater the number of acceptances you'll get. It's a numbers game.

Step 4. Once you're connected with someone, you'll be able to view all the connections that they've made. These pages are great to explore since you already have a contact in common. You can offer these people the opportunity to join your network as well. While this can be a great deal of fun, be careful. Some people find this activity to be so addictive that they end up spending too much time at it and neglect their business.

Step 5. Repeat at facebook.com and at myspace.com.

Case Study

Bob Herrera, vice president of sales & marketing for the Ralph Nichols Group, was tired of going door-to-door making sales calls. Although he was extremely successful at it, this cold-calling was taking up too much of his time. He was looking for a way to streamline the process of turning cold leads into warm leads, so he could spend his time speaking with people who were interested in his products and who represented a greater likelihood of making a sale.

I encouraged Bob to create pages on both MySpace and LinkedIn, and spend a few hours each week building his network and making connections with local businesses. In just a matter of weeks, Bob's network grew. Not only did he get appointments with people who were interested in his products, but his new contacts were the key decision makers as well.

While Bob still hits the pavement making cold calls, he now integrates online networking into his sales strategy. His tired feet thank him for this, and his bank account has swelled!

Resources

myspace.com is the most frequently used networking site on the Web.

linkedin.com is a networking site targeted to the business world.

facebook.com was once exclusive to college students, but it is now open to the public.

twitter.com is one of the latest sites to crash the social networking party. Here, you post single-sentence updates about you and/or your company and you can see other people's posts by becoming their follower.

Web Tidbit

You've got a friend in me! Go to linkedin.com/in/coreyperlman or http://profile.to/coreyperlman/ and make a connection with me. Just let me know that you read my book and I'll happily invite you into my network of friends and colleagues. You can also connect with me on twitter by searching @coreyperlman. See you in cyberspace!

CHAPTER 11

ARTICLES

Be known as a content expert in your field and allow others to market your web site for you.

In this chapter, you will learn:

Why articles are critical to increasing traffic to your web site.
How articles can positively affect your search engine ranking.
Tips to maximize the effectiveness of your articles.
The exact steps to create the perfect article.

I recently had a conversation with a friend who was looking to brand himself as a fitness and health expert. He had been to a few of my workshops and had a list of ten steps he wanted to implement. He had some work ahead of him and wanted to know where he should start. He had a three-hour plane trip coming up, and I told him his goal was to write a 400 to 600-word article before the plane touches down in California. In this article, he was to provide valuable tips and recommendations to help his audience become healthier. I told him to pack as much value in that article as he could and to not be afraid to give his secrets away. I explained that the more value he included in the article, the greater the chance that his readers would become addicted to his content and become hungrier for more.

Writing articles is an excellent way to brand yourself as an expert in your field and increase your chances of appearing in the major search engines. Obviously, your first step is to write the article, and there are a few guidelines you should follow. First, make sure your title is intriguing and catchy. You will be up against thousands of other articles in your field, and you want to separate yourself from the competition. Next, provide real value in your article. I like to use the "Five Points" method, where I give away five actions, tips, or points in one article. If I was writing about becoming healthier, I might write about the five ways to increase your stamina and energy during the workday.

Next, I soft-sell something about my business. Again, if becoming healthier is my topic, I might talk about my three-month boot camp where I've helped hundreds of people improve their diet and lose weight. Finally, my bio always ends the article. I inform my readers why I have the credibility to be writing about this topic. I then end with a link to my web site and my email address.

Now that the article is complete, it is time to get it to the masses. I post my articles using multiple online article submission web sites. Web sites like articlealley.com will allow you to submit your article to their database for free. When you submit your article to these distribution web sites, your article becomes its own web page. As you recall from previous chapters, search engines evaluate content of web pages to decide where to place them on their site. Because your article is nothing but content and houses a great number of keywords, it is very attractive to search engines. Then you rinse and repeat. Keep writing articles and keep submitting them to the same web sites. Since the article submission resources I'll provide you are all free, the only cost is your time. And it is time well spent! Articles have made a major impact on search engines over the past few years. With some searches, the results can come back with as many articles as actual web sites. Remember, the name of this game is to increase your odds of showing up on a search engine. And one of the best ways to do this is by writing multiple articles that become their own web pages.

The other way to get your article to the masses is to allow others to use your article in their online publications. There are literally thousands of businesses that make their livelihood by promoting user-driven content. If they believe that your article will add value to their site, they'll use it, and, in return, will list you and your web site as the source of the content.

Web sites like ezinearticles.com allow others to access your article to use in their e-newsletters, blogs, and so on. Of course, they'll insist that those who use your article cite you and your web site as the source of the article. The more content rich your articles are, the better the chance that you'll be picked up by others who want to use your content. Your articles will always include a link to your web site and, therefore, create instant link popularity for your site (see Chapter 6 for a discussion of link popularity).

Here's an example of an article:

Tips for Success

No. 1. Add your fab five keywords phrases to all of your articles in order to increase their chances of being picked up by the search engines.

No. 2. Always find time to write articles. You can use them over and over again in multiple sources. I place my articles in my blogs, e-newsletters, web sites, and so on. At a minimum, I suggest writing and submitting one article per month.

No. 3. Make sure to always include a link to your web site in your bio.

No. 4. Make sure to post your articles on your web site before submitting to other distribution sites. This will help search engines understand that this is your content and, therefore, give you credit for it.

Exercise: Create a Template for Your Article

Step 1. Think of the subject you will write about.

Example: Adjusting your diet to become healthier and happier.

_____

_____

_____

Step 2. Create a catchy title.

Example: Find the Fountain of Youth from the Foods You Eat!

_____

Step 3. Come up with five tips or recommendations about your topic.

Example:

1. Eat six small meals a day.

2. Drink at least eight glasses of water.

3. Stay away from carb-heavy lunches.

4. Snack on fruits and veggies instead of candy and sweets.

5. Don't forget to eat breakfast!

_____

_____

_____

_____

_____

Step 4. Write your bio.

Example: Corey Perlman has been a health expert for more than 13 years. He graduated from Ohio State University with a master's degree in sports nutrition and has worked at the Health Institute of Ohio for 11 years. For more info on Corey's next workshop or to hire Corey as a trainer, feel free to visit his web site at www.coreyhealthywayoflife.com.

_____

_____

_____

_____

_____

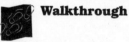 **Walkthrough**

Step 1. Go to ezinearticles.com.
Step 2. Review other articles, and make sure yours is formatted in a similar way.
Step 3. Submit an article to ezinearticles.com.
Step 4. Repeat this process with digg.com.

Case Study

As you know, I'm the author of this book about how to increase search engine rankings. My credibility therefore hinges on my own rankings. When I teach my seminars, I never get through the first session without someone googling my name to see where I rank. I'm pleased to say that they find the majority of the top 50 results are all related to me!

This, however, was not always the case. I encountered a problem with a movie star named Ron Perlman (remember, my last name is Perlman) who was dominating the keyword phrase "Corey Perlman" on the search engines. That was until I started to write articles, and getting them distributed. Due to their wide readership, I now own the majority of search results when my name is searched.

I have to admit that every so often I do get lazy, and another Ron Perlman web site sneaks back into the top 10 results. So back to work I go!

Here's a Google search of my name on Dec 3, 2008:

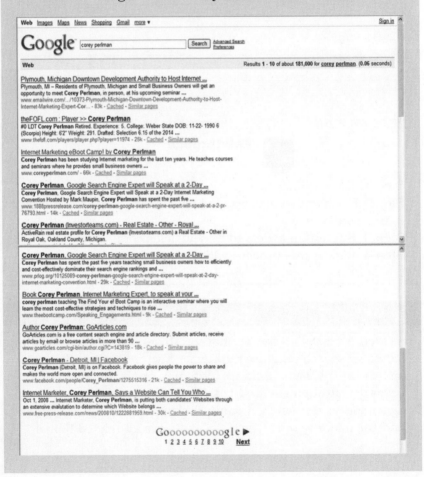

Resources

ezinearticles.com is a free site where you can submit articles for others to use in their e-newsletters. You can also pull articles from this site and use them in your own enewsletter. Just be sure to cite the source.

digg.com is another free site where you can submit an article. Its placement on sites is based upon how many people "digg" it

Web Tidbit

The more sites you add your article to, the better your chance of distributing the article to more readers and seeing them appear on search engines. For my entire list of article submission web sites, go to www.ebootcampbook. com/resources.

CHAPTER 12

PRESS RELEASES

Generate buzz about your products and services and make a huge splash on the search engines.

I'm not sure I completely agree with the old adage that all press is good press. Given the choice, I think we'd all prefer good news about our business over bad. Of course, you can't always control the type of press you receive. The Internet, however, has drastically changed the landscape of news writing and given us more control than ever before. This chapter is dedicated to making you an official press writer for your business.

You get to decide what's newsworthy about your products or services, and write about them. For example, did your company recently celebrate an anniversary? Did you just launch a new product or service? Do you have something to announce that people in your industry would be interested in? All of these events would be great topics for writing a press release.

Once you have a press release written, you need to get them to the right outlets that will create the Internet buzz that you are looking for. One of my favorite sources is emailwire.com. For a small yearly fee, they will blast your press release out to more than 22,000 major and micro news sites. Trust me, it's worth every penny. I've listed other press release distribution sites in the resources section of this chapter.

Not only will press releases create buzz about your business, but they are a highly effective strategy to winning the search-engine game. I've seen some Google searches where the top 10 results were all press releases.

The reason for this search-engine success is, just like an article, a press release is its own web page. One press release can show up on a thousand different news sites. Any of these sites can show up on Google or any other search engine when someone uses keywords that are also found in the press release. That is why it is important to consciously include important keywords in your press releases. By also adding your web site link to each press release that you write, you are creating instant link popularity for your web site. So your press releases can actually be a huge help to increasing your web site's search engine ranking. I'm so excited, my nerd bowtie is actually spinning! I love this stuff!

Here's an example of a press release from pr-inside.com:

Tips for Success

No. 1. Add keywords to all of your press releases in order to increase their chances of being picked up by the search engines.

No. 2. Try to get press releases distributed on a regular basis. At a minimum, I suggest writing and submitting two press releases per month.

No. 3. Use a ghostwriter. If you don't have time to write press releases, find a friend, family member, coworker, or anyone who's a good writer and ask them to write for you.

No. 4. Always include a link to your web site from your press releases.

No. 5. Add your press release to other areas of your web presence.

No. 6. Make sure to post your press release on your web site before submitting to other distribution sites. This will help search engines understand that this is your content and, therefore, give you credit for it.

 Exercise: Create a Template for Your Press Release

Step 1. Create an announcement or headline.

Example: "Faye's Furniture Store Celebrates Its 30th Birthday!"

_____

_____

_____

Step 2. Get a testimonial from a highly satisfied customer.

Example: "Morgan Hart, a shopper in Portland, Oregon, states, 'I was treated warmly and courteously from the moment I was greeted at the door of Faye's Furniture Store. Everyone I spoke with was professional and extremely knowledgeable about the merchandise. I'd recommend Faye's to anyone interested in outstanding service and getting a super deal on quality furniture!'"

Step 3. Develop a "call to action," or what you would like your prospective customers to do.

Example: "Visit Faye's Furniture Store by December 15th, mention this article and receive 15 percent off your total purchase price."

_____

_____

_____

Step 4. Provide a link to your web site so people can get more information about your business.

Example: fayefurniture.com.

_____

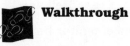 **Walkthrough**

Step 1. Go to free-press-release.com
Step 2. Register on their site. It's free!
Step 3. Start submitting press releases.

Case Study

Philip Lechter has been a friend and a business associate for a long time. He is a very knowledgeable investor and entrepreneur and has made a nice business for himself as a professional speaker and consultant. Philip was looking to increase his presence on the Web, but his greatest challenge was the celebrity status of one of his family members. Because his mother, Sharon Lechter, was the co-author of *Rich Dad Poor Dad,* each time his name was googled, results about Sharon would dominate that page.

We started to write press releases about Phillip each time he'd do a teleseminar or give a speech. Slowly but surely, when Phillip's name was searched on Google, his press releases would appear over all the other results. We accomplished Phillip's goal, and Sharon was happy to let her son share some of the spotlight. Now if Phillip's press releases start to show up when Sharon's name is searched, we might both be in trouble!

Resources

emailwire.com submits an unlimited number of press releases for a flat fee (see the site for the cost).

prweb.com is another press release service (see the site for cost per release prices).

pandia.com/features/pressrelease.html contains an excellent article on the power of using press releases.

elance.com is a great site where you can hire a ghostwriter to help write your press releases. The great thing about this site is elance.com does not release your payment until you are happy with the quality of work.

Web Tidbit

For a complete list of my press release distribution sites, go to ebootcampbook.com/resources.

CHAPTER 13

BLOGS

Your personal online forum to inform people about your products or services and brand yourself as an expert in the field.

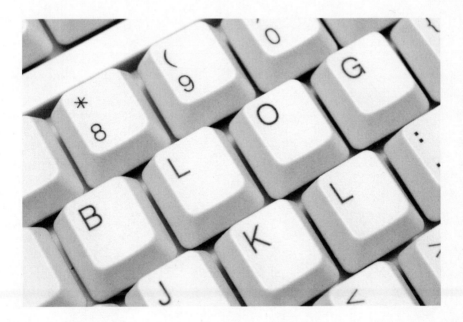

The definition of a blog.

What sites I recommend to create your blog.

How your blog can help increase traffic to your web site
and positively impact your search engine rankings.

In its simplest form, a blog (short for web log) is a web page that provides content for others to see. You can share stories, testimonials, articles, pictures, advertisements, thoughts—whatever your heart desires. You can create the content yourself, or you can republish someone else's work so long as you cite them as the source. Blogs are free to create, easy to maintain, and are powerful tools for winning the search engine game and driving traffic to your web site.

One of the reasons I recommend having a blog as part of your web presence is because it attracts search engines. This is due to the fact that blogs are content heavy and loaded with keywords. So, by having one, you're increasing your chances of being noticed by a search engine when any of your important keywords are searched.

A complaint I sometimes hear is that having a blog show up on a search engine can actually be a negative because it distracts a user from finding the person's actual web site. I believe that as long as your content is showing up—versus a competitor's—you are ultimately winning the game. And don't worry if a user does click on your blog instead of your actual web site. The blog can act

Example of a blog:

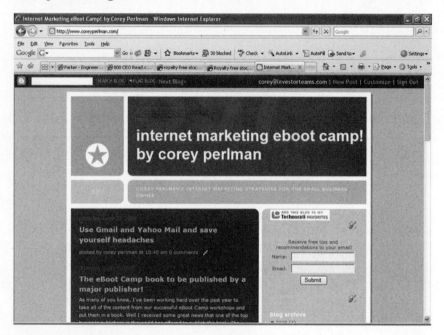

as an introduction to you and your content, and it can lead the person to your web site when they're ready. Remember, the object is not just to appear on a search engine once, but rather to dominate the search results with your content and leave the user no choice but to click on a link to one of your sites.

Along with the important role a blog plays in the search engine game, it can also give you the opportunity to create an online relationship (eRelationship) with customers and potential customers. If you're offering real value, people will be more likely to become frequent visitors of your blog. They also won't hesitate to forward your blog to others who might find the information useful. A well-maintained blog full of desirable content can spread like wildfire as word-of-mouth is still one of the most effective marketing tools on the planet.

So as you start thinking about what to put in your blog, think about what customers and potential customers might find valuable. A sales coach, for example, might include a daily inspirational sales quote. And a golf instructor could offer a daily tip for improving one's golf game. As an Internet marketer, I like to provide weekly web site recommendations that I think my readers will find valuable.

Take some time below to create a framework for your blog.

Tips for Success

No. 1. Use RSS (Real Simple Syndication) feeds. Many news sites and informational sites have RSS feeds that will allow you to use their content in your blog. It's not copy and paste; it's actually easier. If you use the RSS feed for CNN, for example, their Breaking News Report can automatically appear in your blog. You can also set up a RSS feed for information you create so others can automatically receive your content. Use the "help" information on your blogging tool to see how to use RSS feeds.

No. 2. I suggest using blogger.com as your blogging tool of choice. The reason for this is that blogger.com is owned by Google. I figure that if you're trying to get your blog to appear on google.com, why not use the blogging tool that they own.

No. 3. Make sure to "Hurl Your URL" on your blog. This will provide an easy transition for your readers to get to your web site when they're ready.

No. 4. Always include your fab five keyword phrases throughout your blog. Remember, google.com and other search engines look at blogs just like they do web pages, by searching for frequently used keywords and then ranking them accordingly.

No. 5. If you start getting traffic to your blog, consider using Google's advertising tool, AdSense, as a way to create some additional revenue. When you sign up for AdSense, they'll populate your blog with relevant advertisements, and each time one gets clicked on you make money. Google has made it quick and easy to set up and start making money right away! Go to google.com/adsense to learn more.

Exercise: Create a Template for Your Blog

Step 1. Decide on your theme, or what your blog will be about.

Example: Beauty tips for women.

_____

_____

_____

_____

Step 2. Choose a title.

Example: Cosmetology 101.

_____

Step 3. Select your blog URL (web site).

Example: cosmetology101.blog.com

_____

Step 4. Think of a topic for your first post.

Example: Three ways to look younger without spending a
fortune.

_____

 Walkthrough

Step 1. Pick a blogging tool and go to their site. Again, I
suggest blogger.com.

Step 2. Follow the steps for creating your blog, using the
template you just created.

Step 3. Create your first post by introducing your blog and explaining how it can help people.

Step 4. E-mail your blog to 10 people so they can check it out. Also ask them to forward your blog to others who might find it valuable.

Cocktail Information

A "flog" is the term created for a fake blog. These are usually marketing ploys that are set up to look like real, informational blogs, but they're just there to promote and sell products.

A "vlog" is a blog that contains video.

A "log" is a piece of wood that you can use to make a fire or build a cabin. *Author's note: My friend Bill secretly added that last sentence when he edited my book. I thought it was so funny, I left it in. Thanks Bill!*

Web Tidbit

To have a successful blog, you must offer meaningful content and keep your audience engaged. For this web tidbit, I've highlighted some of my favorite Internet marketing blogs. Take note of how often they post content as well as the amount of value they offer their readers. Hopefully you'll gain some inspiration as you begin creating your blog.

mattcutts.com/blog/—Matt works for Google and is a great source for information regarding Google and other Internet marketing topics.

vanessafoxnude.com—Trust me, it's not what you think. This is an authentic Internet marketing blog with great information. Vanessa also has a great sense of humor—evidenced by her URL and subsequent tagline: "What, you were expecting pictures?"

techcrunch.com—This is a very popular blog dedicated to profiling new cutting edge products and companies that are changing the digital landscape. Fascinating information.

debbieweil.com/blog/—The title of her blog is BlogWrite for CEOs. Great blog about what the CEOs and corporate executives of major companies are doing in the world of social networking.

Mattbacak.com—Matt is one of the most successful Internet marketers on the planet. Every time he speaks, I listen . . . and you should too!

Drivingtraffic.com—Ryan Deiss is one of the few Internet marketing gurus out there who gives his most precious secrets away. I'm addicted to his content!

Other great Internet marketing blogs to check out:

seomoz.org/blog

toprankblog.com

marketingpilgrim.com

stuntdubl.com

And if you want my latest recommendations and tips for success, feel free to explore my blog at coreyperlman.com. Sorry, I couldn't help myself.

Resources

Blogger.com is a blogging tool owned by Google.

Wordpress.com is another blogging tool.

http://360.yahoo.com is Yahoo's blogging tool.

google.com/adsense is an introduction to Google's AdSense program, which allows you to earn money by advertising on your blog.

feedblitz.com is an opt-in software that will allow you to capture user info on your blog and then e-mail them information about your products or services.

OPT-IN FORM

*Turn a web site visitor into a
paying customer.*

The definition of an opt-in form.

Why it is critical to have an opt-in form on your web site.

How to ensure people use your opt-in form.

How to avoid costly mistakes that can result in high opt-outs and your e-mail being categorized as spam.

If showing up on a search engine is the cake and getting your link clicked on instead of the others is the icing (the good kind, not that fondant stuff), then having an opt-in form filled out on your web site is the perfect cherry on top! An opt-in form is an area on your web site, or any of your web presence resources, where a person can fill out information, like their name and e-mail address, enabling you to stay connected with them on an ongoing basis.

Once a person has offered their contact information, you can email them about specials, upcoming events, and other information concerning your products or services. You can continue to communicate with them until such time as they decide to opt-out, which means they're asking you to stop e-mailing them. By following some of the guidelines below, you'll keep your opt-outs to a minimum.

I can't stress enough the importance of having an effective opt-in box on your web site. First, without one, you run the risk of people coming to your web site and never knowing who they were and what

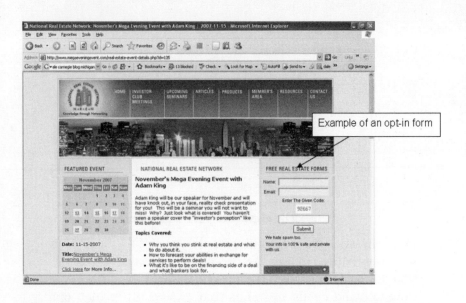

Example of an opt-in form

they wanted—an absolute sin in the Internet marketing world. And just having an opt-in box is not enough. It must be effective, and by being effective, I mean having a high ratio of people opting-in versus leaving your site without providing their information.

It's challenging to have an effective opt-in box because people are very protective of their e-mail address, and rightfully so. Spammers have taken over our e-mail accounts and made us skeptical about many of the e-mails we receive. You must earn a person's trust before they'll give you their e-mail address. And you can do this by assuring them that you won't sell or give it to anyone.

You should also explain exactly why you're asking for someone's e-mail address. If you're planning on sending them special offers on products, for example, explain this clearly in the space provided just above or below your opt-in form.

To encourage people to give you their name and e-mail address, offer something of value in return. This could be a favorite recipe, if you happen to be a restaurant owner, or tips for keeping plants healthy should you be a landscaper. It can be anything you like, so long as your customers will find the information valuable. And don't be afraid to give important information away. The exchange of your content for someone's e-mail will start a relationship between the two of you, and it could result in a customer for life. I'll take that deal every time!

Tips for Success

No. 1. Don't be intrusive with your opt-ins by having one pop up (or float in) as soon as a user visits your web site. Although studies show that these disruptive opt-in forms are effective, I believe that a well-placed box on your homepage, with an enticing offer, will work just as well while not offending anyone.

No. 2. If you find that your opt-in form is not as effective as you'd like, consider moving it to a different part of your homepage. You can also up the ante by adding more value to your offer.

No. 3. Consider using an "auto-responder" along with your opt-in form. This is software that will automatically e-mail people who opt-in on your web site. Although there's a cost to using auto-responders, it will save you time and money in the long run.

 ### Exercise

Step 1. Write the text that will go above your opt-in form to intrigue someone to give you his or her name and e-mail address.

Example: I'm a tennis instructor. If you give me your name and email address, I'll send you monthly tennis tips like the best way to increase the power of your serve.

_____

_____

Step 2. Provide the information you'll be giving to the user.

Example: When tossing the ball in the air, make contact when it's at its peak.

_____

_____

_____

Step 3. Ask your web designer to create an opt-in form for you on your home page, where you'll request a name and e-mail address in exchange for the above information.

Case Study

A few years ago, my friend Eric Tomei suddenly lost his father to a heart attack. Eric was devastated by the loss, but he turned his emotion into a passion to help others to cope with the sudden loss of a parent. He wrote a book, titled *I Miss My Dad*, and created a web site, lostdadsclub.com, to support his book.

Eric wanted to use his web site to build a community for people to share their experiences of loss with the idea that these stories would benefit others. Eric needed a way to collect the names and e-mails of the people who visited his site so he could begin to build his community. We created an opt-in form on his home page, and he offered a free e-newsletter to everyone who opted-in to the community.

I'm proud to say that Eric's acquisition rate for converting users to members is more than 50 percent, and he's well on his way to creating a wonderful community that will benefit thousands of people all over the world.

Resources

clickz.com/showPage.html?page=3498726 is an article on the benefits of using opt-ins on your web site.

aweber.com is my auto-responder site of choice. You can set-up auto-responders to automatically e-mail specific messages to those who opt-in to your web site.

getresponse.com/index/cperlman is another auto-responder site.

CHAPTER 15

E-MAIL MARKETING

Stay "top of mind" with your customers and get them to buy over and over again.

The definition of e-mail marketing.
The tool I recommend using and why.
Why using e-mail marketing is so effective in creating repeat business.
Steps to create the perfect e-mail marketing campaign.

E-mail marketing is an effective way to promote your products or services and stay connected to your customers. Whether you e-mail 10 people or 1,000, using e-mail marketing is a cost-effective way to build brand awareness for your business.

In this strategy, you send e-mails only to people who have requested e-mails from you. If you send e-mails to people blindly, without first having obtained their permission, then those e-mails are considered "spam."

Sending spam is a practice you should stay far away from. Not only do you risk being "blacklisted," which disables your ability to send people or companies e-mails, but it's also unethical and a bad business practice.

In this chapter, you'll learn to create a powerful e-mail marketing campaign the right way, by offering high-value content to people who will be excited to hear from you.

An e-newsletter (or e-zine) is the most common form of e-mail marketing. It's essentially an electronic magazine filled with content about a specific subject that is sent out to a large number of people.

In the previous chapter, we discussed the importance of collecting names and e-mail addresses from people who visit your site. Once you have their e-mails, a great way to stay connected to them is to send periodic e-newsletters. As long as you continue providing valuable content, they'll remain interested in opening and reading your e-newsletter, and that will help to keep your business paramount in your customers' minds.

Here's an example of an e-newsletter:

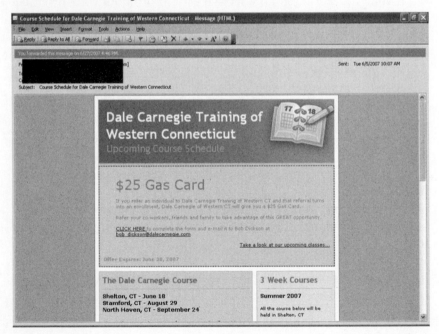

Using an e-newsletter service like Constant Contact (constant-contact.com) is important because it can offer features that standard email tools, such as Outlook or Google mail, can't.

Constant Contact enables you to track the effectiveness of your email by providing detailed reports on the activity you had for a particular campaign. These reports will contain crucial information, including how many people are opening your e-newsletters and how many are not receiving your e-mails because the messages were blocked by spam filters or the e-mail address you're using is incorrect.

You can also track the effectiveness of links that you've included in your e-newsletters by monitoring how many people clicked on them. For example, if your e-newsletter contained a link to your web site, you could see precisely how many people clicked on the link along with their contact information. This will enable you to make adjustments to your e-newsletter by moving links to a different location or changing content to improve the effectiveness of your campaign. Also, if the person clicked on a link to a specific product or service you offer, you could call or e-mail that individual with additional information.

Here's an example of Constant Contact's reporting tool:

The information below will show you how to begin creating your e-newsletter and start the process of becoming familiar with the email marketing tool of your choice.

Tips for Success

No. 1. Evaluate the effectiveness of your e-newsletters, and make changes accordingly. For example, if you're not happy with the number of people who opened your newsletter, try changing the subject line or sending it out on a different day.

No. 2. Be careful about the amount of selling you do in your enewsletters. If you overdo it, you'll frustrate your audience. Provide value first, and your readers will be more accepting of a "soft sell" down the road.

No. 3. Add an opt-in form to your web site to increase membership to your e-newsletter. Add the same opt-in form to your blog as well.

No. 4. Make sure you have an opt-out option in your e-newsletter. This is required by most e-mail marketing web sites, and it lowers the risk of being reported as spam.

No. 5. All together now, "Hurl Your URL!" Put your web site address in an obvious place, and let your readers know that they can click on it anytime to buy your products or services.

Exercise: Create a template for your enewsletter

Step 1: Who is it from? (You can choose to send the e-mail from your name or your business.)

Example: Bill's New and Used Bookstore

Step 2. Who's your target customer?

Example: People who left their name and e-mail address at Bill's New and Used Bookstore.

_____

Step 3. What's your subject?

Example: Best-selling books of the month.

_____

Step 4. List three headlines that relate to the subject.

Example: An editorial review of the top three best-selling books.

_____

_____

_____

Step 5. What's your call to action? It should be something that will encourage a user to go to your web site.

Example: To see the reviews of these books or to make a purchase, click on the link to visit our web site.

_____

_____

Step 6. Add some links to partnership web sites. By referring business to other sites, you can receive revenue by being an affiliate of their products or services. They may also be more willing to add your link to their web site or enewsletter.

Example: troychamberofcommerce.com or dalescoffeehouse.com.

_____

_____

_____

Step 7. Create a coupon for one of your products or services.

Example: Print out this coupon and bring it to the store to get 10 percent off of your next purchase.

_____

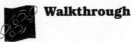 **Walkthrough**

Step 1. Choose an e-newsletter tool (see Resource section), and go to its web site.
Step 2. Sign up for the free trial. (If the site you're on doesn't have a free trial, try another resource.)
Step 3. Become comfortable using their e-newsletter layout by creating a practice campaign.
Step 4. Send the practice e-newsletter to 10 people, and ask them to provide feedback.
Step 5. Once you feel you're ready, create a real e-newsletter and send it to your customer list.

Case Study

Bob Dickson, the owner of the Dale Carnegie franchise in western Connecticut, was trying to attract more people to his sales, leadership, and personal development courses. He knew that the best way to generate more interest would be for graduates to talk with colleagues and friends about their achievements and breakthroughs.

Bob decided to create a monthly e-newsletter filled with great tips and reminders of all the benefits graduates have gained from taking his courses.

This kept the Dale Carnegie name at "top of mind" for the hundreds of people who received Bob's e-newsletter. They'd talk about the course with coworkers and friends, and even forward the e-newsletter to other people who could benefit from the content.

Bob quickly started receiving phone calls from qualified leads, and these leads turned into new enrollments for his courses. By creating an e-newsletter, Bob found an easy and cost-effective way to stay in touch with his graduates and keep them talking about the benefits of Dale Carnegie training.

Resources

constantcontact.com (Go to http://tinyurl.com/cp123 for my co-branded Constant Contact page) is an e-newsletter tool that I use and highly recommend.
swiftpage.com is another excellent e-newsletter tool.
ftc.gov/spam/ provides information about spam rules and regulations.

Web Tidbit

I spend (and my wife would agree) too many weekends at Internet marketing seminars and workshops staying current with the latest and most effective marketing strategies. The "eBoot Camp eTip" is a bi-weekly e-mail filled with the latest Internet marketing resources and recommendations you need to stay competitive in an ever-evolving digital world. To sign up for the free "eBoot Camp eTip," go to www.ebootcampbook.com/etips.

CHAPTER 16

VIDEO

One of the hottest Internet marketing strategies and easier than you think to get started.

In this chapter, you will learn:

Why video has become the hottest Internet marketing tool
   on the planet.
The step-by-step process to getting video on the Internet.
Where to share your video for maximum viewing.
How to maximize the effectiveness of your videos.

As we all know, the Internet is an ever-evolving animal, and if you blink for even a second, you might miss the newest innovation or technology breakthrough. I joke with my clients that if they want to stay current with the latest Internet marketing trends, just ask a teenager. They knew the power of social networking sites long before we did, and the same goes for video.

Generation Y helped make YouTube.com the latest craze on the Internet. They've been actively using the video-sharing site for years now. Only just recently have we discovered its value as both a networking tool and search engine powerhouse. Sites like Youtube.com have made it easy for anyone, and I mean anyone, to post videos for the public to view. All you need is a video recorder, and last I checked, you could pick one up at Target or Best Buy for under $100.

So there are two questions that might be running through your head right now: why should you even bother with this and, if I can safely get past that question, what type of videos should you record.

Let's start with the first question. I can think of two power-ful reasons why it is worth creating video around your products or services. The first reason is because media outlets (specifi-cally video) are where people are spending their time surfing these days. According to a study by comScore, 138 million users, or three in four U.S. Internet users, viewed a video in November 2007. A wise man once told me that you can't dictate the market; you must let the market dictate you. So if Internet users are head-ing toward video as their medium of choice, then let's meet half-way by having videos about you and your business on display.

The second reason is because video links are becoming a pow-erful weapon in winning the search engine game. All of the major search engines are looking for ways to provide a more personal-ized, richer experience for their users. It's no wonder that Google was quick to acquire YouTube.com back in 2006. They knew video would be a major part of the search engine experience moving forward. When you upload a video to YouTube, they ask you for keywords that describe your video. When those words are typed in Google, your video has a good chance of being listed in the results.

So hopefully I've provided enough evidence for you to at least consider adding video to your Internet marketing campaign. Now let's talk about what you should record. One way to use video is to shoot advertisements about your products or services. If some-one is on Google searching for a product or service and they come across a video of you discussing the product or service and its benefits, they might be inclined to watch. At the end of the short video, you will direct them to your web site to buy.

Another suggestion is something you may have already cre-ated in a previous chapter. Take the "five things" you wrote about in one of your articles and record them on video. Make the video less than five minutes and pack it full of value. At the end of the segment, "Hurl Your Url" by announcing your web address. You might even offer a special incentive just for your video audience to encourage them to buy now.

In summary, if it's of value to other people, then it's worthy of a video. The viral opportunities that come with sharing video is something the likes of which this Internet marketer has never seen. Perhaps the best example of this is the "Will it Blend?"

phenomenon that swept the globe in 2008. Blendtec (a blender manufacturer) put out some videos on YouTube of them blending all sorts of outrageous things like glow sticks, rakes and the most famous of all: an iPhone. This video alone received over 10 million views and has made Blendtec an Internet success overnight. But did it translate into sales? You bet it did. They're up over 400 percent on household blender sales. Now your video doesn't have to be funny enough for America's Funniest Home Videos or inspiring enough to be on the Oprah Winfrey Show, it just needs to provide valuable information that people will enjoy watching. You never know, you could be the next Blendtec!

Tips for Success

No. 1. There are many camcorders you can buy to shoot your videos. The Flip Video from theflip.com is $100–150 and shoots quality video that is easily uploaded to your computer. Give it a try!

No. 2. Remember to always include your web site address at the end of your videos. It's great to say it, but even better when it appears on the video screen.

No. 3. Don't make your videos more than five minutes long. Attention spans are at a premium these days, and I haven't found one that will stay and watch for more than five minutes.

Walkthrough

Step 1. Go to YouTube.com.

Step 2. In the search bar, type in "sales tips."

Step 3. Watch one or two videos (under five minutes) and observe what you like and don't like about each of them.

Step 4. What did you like?

Step 5. What did you dislike?

Exercise

Step 1. Research camcorders and pick one that is right for you. Again, I gave you one example (flipvideo.com), but do your own research and pick the one that is right for you.

Step 2. Decide the type of video you will shoot (advertisement, instructional, informational, etc.).

Example: I will be doing an instructional video on how to properly demo a bathroom.

_____

Step 3. Write the script for your video.

Example: Hello and thank you for taking a few minutes with me to go through the process of demolishing a bathroom. The first step is taking safety precautions to make sure you don't get hurt. You should wear safety goggles and gloves during the entire project.

(Fast forward to ending).

I want to thank you taking the time to watch this video and if you'd like to see more videos or sign up for one of our classes, please visit our web site at (insert URL).

_____

_____

_____

_____

_____

Step 4. Post your video to YouTube.com. For assistance, go to google.com/support/youTube/.

Resources

youtube.com is a free web site where you can post videos and search for videos on a vast variety of topics.

camtasia.com is a software you can buy that will record screenshots from your computer while you provide the voiceover. This is great if you want to record a Power Point presentation and put it on YouTube.com.

myspacetv.com is Myspace.com's place for sharing videos.

willitblend.com/videos.aspx?type=unsafe&video=iphone3g is the Blendtek video of their CEO blending an iPhone. A must see!

Case Study

As a sales trainer and motivational speaker, John Rodgers needed a strong Internet presence. John has a great reputation of inspiring crowds with his passion and enthusiasm for helping people. I was able to witness that first hand at a convention where he was one of the keynote speakers. John received a standing ovation, and people talked about his speech throughout the rest of the convention.

When John asked me how he could expand his presence on the Web in hopes of helping more people, my first question was "Do you have a recording of that speech?" Two weeks later I received a digital copy of John's powerful talk, and I immediately uploaded it to YouTube.com.

In just a few months, John had more than 1,000 viewers, and he has seen the video show up on Google with numerous keyword phrases. These results are without e-mailing any of his colleagues or friends, and are driven just by curious Internet surfers who found his video interesting. John has found a brand new medium to get his passion and enthusiasm out to the masses quickly and, since YouTube.com is a free service, cost-effectively.

Cocktail Information

Early in 2005, Chad Hurley, Steve Chen, and Jawed Karim were working at PayPal.com. As the story goes, they were having difficulty e-mailing a video clip and came up with a video sharing web site to resolve that issue. The guys bought their domain name and opened their video sharing web site to the public. It spread like wildfire, and soon they received two rounds of funding from Sequoia Capital. On October 9, 2006, Google acquired the company for $1.65 billion in a stock-for-stock transaction. It is said that there are more than 100 million videos watched a day on this site, and it's the fourth most accessed web site in the world. And the web site is, of course, (insert me doing a drum roll with my fingers on my keyboard) YouTube.com!

CHAPTER 17

WEB SITE USABILITY

Turn your web site into a dynamic sales and marketing machine.

You've done it! By learning how to win the search engine game
and create a powerful web presence, you've set yourself up for a
dramatic increase in web site traffic.

The final step is to make sure your web site is in perfect form
and ready to receive all this new traffic. Your objective is to deliver
a clear message to your users and have them act on whatever
your desired result might be.

The challenge with many web sites is that the web designer
built the site for you, as you are their customer. They didn't take
into account the importance of meeting the needs of *your customer.* For this reason, some sites look attractive, but lack important content that your users are searching for. Others convey the
perfect message, but that message is lost by too many images or
pictures that dominate the site.

While you hire a web site designer because of his or her
expertise in designing a site, this person most likely isn't knowledgeable about your business. He or she won't know the types of

users coming to your site nor, certainly, the information they're looking for.

Therefore, you must work closely with your designer in the creation and layout of your web site. In the event that your site is already up and running, then you should reevaluate it and make changes and improvements where necessary. Your goal is to have a search engine ready, aesthetically pleasing site that's simple for customers and potential customers to navigate and use. Here are some factors to consider.

With web site design, I like to employ the less-is-more theory. Be judicious in your use of images, include them only when needed since they can be distracting and also slow down the time it takes for a customer to view your site.

As far as color is concerned, I recommend a white background with black text and no more than three primary colors throughout.

The main navigation bar for your web site should contain from five to eight links, and those links should be descriptive enough so users will know exactly where they're going before they actually click on the link. So if it's a link for directions to your store, for example, the link should read "Store Directions" or "Map and Directions."

Your most important content should reside "above the fold," meaning the content that shows up on your computer screen when someone arrives at your web site. "Below the fold" is information that can be seen only by scrolling down to find it. A store address and phone number are good examples of key information that should always be above the fold. And if the primary function of your web site is to sell products, then your "Buy Now" button should be clearly displayed above the fold. Never make a user search for vital information.

Steve Krug, author of the fantastic web site design book *Don't Make Me Think*, created a great activity to test the simplicity and usability of a web site. He suggests picking a random page on your web site and sharing it with a complete stranger. Then ask this person if they can decipher what that particular page is about and also determine what the entire web site is about. This is a great exercise because it's important to keep parts of your site consistent so someone can easily understand who you are and what you sell, no matter what page they are on. Also from any page within your site, they should be able to easily get back to your home page, or navigate to any other part of your web site.

The last matter to discuss is the cost of having a web site designed.

The question small-business owners ask me more than any other is, "How much should I pay for a web site?"

My response to this question is always the same: "What are you looking to accomplish online?" I ask this because price can't even be considered until the client's needs are fully understood.

If a web designer gives you a price before asking you what you want to achieve online, I recommend that you proceed with extreme caution. Depending on the goals you've set for your site and the needs of your customers, the fee can range from literally nothing to several thousand dollars.

There are actually two different types of web sites, each with its own purpose.

The web site you're probably most familiar with is called a "multi-paged" site. It usually consists of six to eight pages with a home page and sub-pages such as "About Us," "Maps and Directions," "Contact Us," and so on. This is the site that most businesses use.

The other site is called a "one-page web site" or "brochure site," and its purpose is usually just to sell products or services. You've undoubtedly seen this type of site when surfing on the Internet. It's quite distinguishable by its long length and content-heavy web page with usually only one link: the Buy Now button. While many people consider this type of site to be obnoxious and ugly, it's often quite effective. To see hundreds of examples, go to Google.com and search the site web-purchases.com.

If all you're looking for is to put your phone number and e-mail address on the Internet, you don't even need to hire a web designer. You can go to yahoo.com or godaddy.com and quickly create a web site for yourself, and at no charge.

But if you want a more robust site, say with six different pages, pictures of your retail store and a spot to post your product line, then you could easily pay $500 or more. If you want to add video, a content management system, or an online store, the cost could then exceed $1,000.

In some cases, you might find you do not even need a web site at all. Yes, you read that correctly, despite the fact that I'm in the web site business.

Notice I said that you might not need a *web site.* I did not say *web pages.* There's a difference between the two. Some of the chapters in this book will have helped you to create resources such as blogs, articles, and press releases. These vital marketing tools will become web pages, and they'll serve many of the same functions as a web site. For example, they can give you a presence on search engines, sell your products and services, and even get people to call you on the phone or come into your store. And the best part of this is that you can create these web pages for free!

Bottom line: When it's time to develop a web site, always begin with your desired outcome for that site. You'll end up saving money and reduce the chance of being disappointed with the result.

Here's an example of a multi-paged site designed using the techniques outlined above.

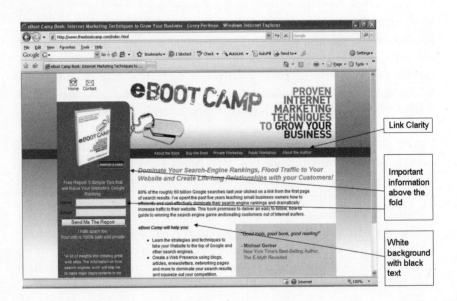

Tips for Success

No. 1. Ask your web designer to make sure your site can be viewed clearly in all browsers. With so many options today (Firefox, Safari, Opera, etc.), you want to be certain that everyone can see your web site in its correct form.

No. 2. When linking to another site, make sure a new window opens up so the user can return to your site with ease.

No. 3. This is a personal pet peeve. If one of the links on your site is a PDF (Portable Document Format) document, indicate this next to the link. This way, a user can decide whether or not to open the document, and you won't run the risk of frustrating someone due to the lengthy time it can take for a PDF to open.

No. 4. Don't spend too much money on hosting your web site. If it's a simple six- to eight-page informational site, you shouldn't pay more than $15 a month for hosting.

No. 5. Remember to spell-check your entire web site.

Case Study

The National Real Estate Network (NREN), a real estate investment club in southeastern Michigan, was looking for ways to boost participation in its monthly events. Getting more traffic to its web site was important, but helping current users find the information they were looking for both quicker and more effectively was the main priority.

I met with the owner of NREN, Mark Maupin, and mapped out a plan that included a total revamp of his web site and the addition of meta tags to help the search engines find the site. Mark indicated that the majority of their users were looking for directions to the venue and information about the speaker for the upcoming event. Together, we moved this key information above the fold so users didn't have to scroll to find it. We also made the navigation links more understandable and easier so users could find additional information regarding the upcoming event and speaker.

These changes made an immediate impact, with participation in events jumping more than 50 percent the first year!

 Walkthrough

Step 1. Browse the home page of a competitor's web site.
Step 2. List two things you like about the site:

_____

_____

Step 3. List two improvements you'd like to make to the site:

_____

_____

Step 4. Browse through the site, and stop somewhere in the middle. Can you get back to the home page? From this page alone, do you clearly understand what this web site is all about?

Exercise: Evaluate Your Web Site

Conduct the exercise below to evaluate the aesthetics and usability of your web site. If you need assistance in any area, use the information that appears below the item being evaluated. Skip any questions that don't apply to your business.

Web Site Evaluation

General

Color pollution _____ No _____ Yes

When a web site contains too many colors it distracts from the site's content. As a result, if you have more than three colors on a particular web page, it's called "color pollution."

Search-Engine Readiness

Title tag	_____ No	_____ Yes
Keywords	_____ No	_____ Yes
Meta description tag	_____ No	_____ Yes

Search engines collect this information and use it as a means of judging a site's relevance to a user's search criteria.

Link popularity _____ (0–5) _____ (6–15) _____ (>16)

The more web sites that have a link to your site, the better.

Multiple domains _____ (0) _____ (1 or 2) _____ (>3)

Besides your main web site address, count the other domain names you own that redirect to your web site. As explained earlier, having multiple domain names is important in winning the search engine game.

Navigation

Links above the fold _____ No _____ Yes

Everything you see when you first land on a web site is information that is "above the fold." There's a significant drop in click-throughs (the amount of times people click on a link) when people have to scroll down to find a link. Keep important information, such as links, high enough on your web site so people don't have to scroll to find it.

Link clarity _____ No _____ Yes

Without clicking on a link, the user should be able to know exactly where he or she is going.

Content

Privacy/policy statement _____ No _____ Yes

This is a statement or link at the bottom of the home page that details any copyright or privacy rules that you have for your site.

Mailing address _____ No _____ Yes
E-mail address _____ No _____ Yes
Phone numbers _____ No _____ Yes

When appropriate, make sure that your mailing address, e-mail address, and phone number are clearly displayed on your web site.

Different page titles _____ No _____ Yes

At the top of the browser, there should be a different title for each page of the web site.

Location with maps or directions _____ No _____ Yes

If you have customers who visit your store, there should be a separate page that provides a map with directions.

Inventory catalog _____ No _____ Yes

If you discuss or show products on your web site, you should have a catalog for this merchandise, and it should be updated on a regular basis.

Store hours _____ No _____ Yes

If customers visit your place of business, make sure to clearly display your store hours on your home page.

Affiliate links _____ No _____ Yes

If you link to a web site that sells products, make sure that you're set up to be paid a commission for every product that's sold to someone who came from your web site.

Subscriber area/opt-in form _____ No _____ Yes

As discussed in Chapter 14, a great way to stay connected to people who visit your web site is by having a subscriber area or opt-in form on your home page.

Navigation bar on every page _____ No _____ Yes

Each page within your web site should have the same navigation bar as your home page.

Speed

Download time _____ (>10 sec.) _____ (5–10 sec.) _____ (<5 sec.)

This is the amount of time it takes for the entire web page to appear on someone's computer screen. Use this link, http://websiteoptimization.com/services/analyze/, to test your site's speed.

E-mail/phone response _____ (1 day or more) _____ (same day) _____ (<1 hr.)

This is the time it takes for you to respond to a question from a user on your web site. Good customer service can be the difference between receiving a compliment or a complaint.

Bonus

Shopping cart _____ No _____ Yes

If you sell multiple products or services on your web site, you should have a shopping cart feature that makes it easy for a user to buy more than one product or service. A good resource for acquiring this functionality is 1shoppingcart.com.

Credit card ready   _____ No   _____ Yes

Again, if you sell products or services on your web site, you should have a safe, secure area to allow users to enter their credit card information. Paypal.com or 1shoppingcart.com are good resources for this service.

   After you've evaluated your web site, make the necessary changes to those areas where you scored poorly.

Resources

webpagesthatsuck.com nominates the worst web sites on the Web, and it is a good resource for things NOT to do.
www.websiteoptimization.com/services/analyze/ can be used to test the download speed of your web site.

Web Tidbit

To receive a downloadable version of the web site evaluation form, go to www.ebootcampbook.com/webeval.

CLOSING WORD

Congratulations! I'm proud to present you with the title of Internet Marketing Superhero!

This is not an easy book to digest and I commend you for reaching the finish line. I'm sure your mind is racing with to-do lists, and you might not know where to begin. My advice is to just start with one action a week. Maybe this week you will set up your blog or your LinkedIn page or create your keyword list. It doesn't matter where you start, it just matters that you start. Commit to at least one action a week. Before you know it, these actions will turn into habit, and you will start seeing results. Don't get frustrated. One blog post won't get you to the top of Google. You need to stay consistent and keep publishing content. The search engines will catch on eventually. And always remember to tweak when needed. If your web site is not performing the way you want it to, change your keywords or your home page content or something else. Play with it until you start seeing more traffic flow through your web site and into your store or office.

I sincerely hope you've enjoyed this Internet-marketing journey and have gained valuable tools to help you grow your business. If I've left any question for you unanswered, please go to ebootcampquestion.com and submit your question. I will make every attempt to answer all the questions I receive. I'd also love to hear from you on how you're progressing using the tools outlined in this book. Please visit my web site at Ebootcampbook.com and send me updates on your progress.

Finally, this techie book wouldn't be complete unless it ended with a quote from *Star Wars'* Yoda. So I'll leave you with my favorite one as you put down the book and start to take action on creating a powerful web presence for your small business:

"Do or Do Not. There is No Try." Yoda.

GLOSSARY

AdWords. Google's flagship product, these are words on web pages that are advertisements, and site owners are paid each time an ad is clicked on them.

Blog. An online journal where you can post content for others to read.

Bot. Shorthand for "robot," an automated program that collects information from web servers regarding the web sites it hosts. The Bot returns the information that's catalogued by the originating search engine.

BPS. Abbreviation for "bits per second," which is a measurement of how fast data are moved from one place to another. For example, a 56k modem can move 56,000 bits per second. Connection speeds are always referred to in terms of bits, not bytes.

Browser. A software program, such as Netscape or Explorer, that views web page content.

Click-through. The action of clicking on a link.

Click-through rate (CTR). The ratio of click-throughs to total emails sent.

Crawler. An automated software agent that's part of a search engine. See "spider-based search engines" for more information.

DNS. Abbreviation for Domain Name System, Domain Name Service, and Domain Name Server. This is an Internet service that translates domain names into numerical IP addresses.

Because domain names consist of letters, they're easy to remember. However, the Internet is based on IP addresses (see definition below) that consist of numbers. Therefore, every time you use a domain name, a DNS service must translate the name into the corresponding IP address. For example, the domain name example.com might translate into 198.105.232.4.

Domain name.   A name that identifies one or more IP addresses. For example, the domain name microsoft.com represents about a dozen IP addresses. Domain names are used in URLs to identify particular web pages. For example, in the URL http://www.ebootcampbook.com, the domain name is ebootcampbook.com.

Hyperlink.   Words or images that, when clicked on, take a user to a different part of a web page or web site. A hyperlink can also take a user to a completely different web site or start the download process of a file.

Hit.   A single request from a web browser for a single item from a web server. If a browser requests a web page that contains six graphics, seven hits are registered by the server: one hit for the page itself and a hit for each of the six graphics.

Home page.   The first page of a web site.

HTML.   Abbreviation for "Hypertext Markup Language," which is the code, or special tags, used to create the basic web page structure.

http:// (always lower case and proceeded by a colon and two forward slash marks) stands for "Hypertext Transfer Protocol," which is the protocol for moving files across the Web. A web address begins with "http://" because the servers use http to deliver the content. However, when typing a web address, you need not type "http://" because your computer will do this for you automatically.

Human-powered search engines.   Engines that rely on humans to submit information that's subsequently indexed and catalogued. Only information that's submitted is put into the index. ChaCha.com is an example of a human-powered search engine.

Internet.   A collective noun that refers to the interconnection of many backbone networks and subnetworks that all use TCP/IP to transport data.

IP address. An identifier for a computer. The format of an IP address is a 32-bit numeric address written as four numbers separated by periods. Each number can be from zero to 255. For example, 1.160.10.240 could be an IP address.

ISP. Abbreviation for "Internet Service Provider," which is a company, such as AOL, that resells its bandwidth from an Internet backbone to home or business users. ISPs also tend to offer hosting and related Internet services, such as e-mail.

Keywords. A word used by a search engine in its search for relevant web pages.

Meta description tag. This is the feature that allows you to influence the description of your web page in the crawlers that support the tag. It's where Google gets the summary about your web page.

Meta tags. Your keywords, title tag, and meta description tag make up your meta tags. Many search engines use this information when building their indices.

OS. Abbreviation for "operating system," which is the software that manages a computer's basic processing. For example, Windows XP is an operating system.

Opt-in. The action of agreeing to receive e-mails from a person, company, or organization by subscribing to an e-mail list.

Opt-out. A mailing list that transmits e-mails to people who have not subscribed to them and lets these people "opt-out" from the list. The subscribers' email addresses may be harvested from the Web, USENET, or other mailing lists. ISP policies and some regional laws consider this equivalent to spamming.

Page views. A unit of measurement referring to how many times a web page has been viewed. If an individual looks at a page five different times, that's still counted as five page views.

Pay-per-click. In online advertising, this term refers to when a site owner is paid each time an ad is clicked on by a user.

Pixel. A unit of measurement used to specify a monitor's resolution. A pixel is one dot on a computer screen. The majority of computer monitors are set to a resolution of 800 pixels wide by 600 pixels tall.

POP. Abbreviation for "post office protocol," a mechanism for retrieving e-mail from a server and delivering it to an e-mail client, such as MS Outlook or Express.

Search engine. A directory of Internet content. There are three types of search engines: spiders (also known as crawlers), human-powered, and a hybrid of the two. Some popular search engines are google.com, yahoo.com, and msn.com.

Search Engine Optimization (SEO) companies. A company that's hired to help your web site rank higher on the most popular search engines using your most important keywords.

Shopping cart. Software used to create an online "storefront," or e-commerce web site. The software acts as a virtual shopping cart, keeping track of items that visitors have ordered and allowing them to add or remove items as desired.

Spam. Junk e-mail that's usually in the form of advertising and is inappropriately sent to a mailing list.

Spider-based search engines. Engines that use automated software agents (called crawlers) that visit a web site to read its content and meta tags. Some also follow the links that the site connects to test its popularity. The crawler returns all that information to a central depository, where the data is indexed. The crawler will periodically return to the sites to check for any information that has changed. The frequency with which this happens is determined by the administrator of the search engine.

Title tag. The headline that describes your web site and is used by search engines as the blue link for your site. You can view your title tag by looking at the very top of your browser or by looking in the source code of that web page.

TLD. Abbreviation for "top-level domain," referring to the suffix attached to Internet domain names. There are a limited number of predefined suffixes, and each one represents a top-level domain. Current top-level domains include:

com - commercial businesses, which is the most common TLD
gov - U.S. government agencies
edu - educational institutions, such as colleges
org - organizations, usually nonprofit
mil - military
net - network organizations

Unique visitor. This is the unit of measurement that most small business owners care about. It indicates how many people came to their web site during a certain period of time. Ask your hosting company or web designer to provide you with monthly reports on your unique visitors.

URL. Abbreviation for "Uniform Resource Locator," the standard way to display an address on the Web. In the example below, the URL includes the protocol (http://) and the domain (ebootcampbook.com).

Example: http://www.ebootcampbook.com

Web or www. This is the World Wide Web, which commonly refers to the massive, global collection of hypertext (http) servers that allow concurrent viewing of Internet data.

BONUS RESOURCES

These links (and more!) can be found at www.ebootcampbook.com/resources

searchenginewatch.com. This web site has everything you need to know about search engines, how they work, and how to improve your ranking.

Webopedia.com. A great resource for anything you want to know about your computer or the Internet.

icann.org. An organization that handles domain name ownership cases among other things.

linkpopularity.com. This web site will tell you how many other web sites contain links to yours.

techeez.com/windows_tips/bits_in_a_byte.htm provides information on how many bits are in a byte, bytes in a kilobyte, and so on.

webhostingratings.com/hostdir.html lists hundreds of hosting sites to host your web site.

dslreports.com/stest will test the speed of your Internet connection.

mydomain.com is one of the hosting sites I've used and recommend.

baragainwebstuff.com provides good deals on hosting plans, domain names, and web sites.

websiteoptimization.com/services/analyze/ will test your web site speed, and provide recommendations on how to improve it.

lyris.com/resources/contentchecker/index.html will analyze your email for potential spam words and phrases.

visualroute.com/ will test the speed of the connection between your computer and the server you're working from. You can also watch how many stops your server request makes on its way to getting you the web page you specified.

thelist.com is a great resource of ISPs in your area.

doubleclick.com is an eMarketing resource with a ton of valuable and free information.

ezinearticles.com lists articles you can use in your ezine.

constantcontact.com is another e-mail marketing tool. This site offers an excellent live demo and a 60-day free trial.

webpagesthatsuck.com is a site dedicated to web pages you *don't* want to emulate.

justtext.com/menu-program-list/program-tasks.html will explain all .exe programs in your task bar, and if they are safe or not.

e-zinez.com/handbook/template.html provides guidelines for creating ezines.

groundbreak.com provides cost-effective, affiliate software that will enable you to let others sell your products, and also track sales, commissions, and so on.

bestcommercetools.com provides a one-stop shop for building web sites and performing search optimization.

monsterwebpromotion.com/web-promotion-tools.asp is a fantastic, free site for analyzing your keyword density, link popularity, search-engine placement and more!

komando.com is America's "Digital Goddess!" She has great information on any techie question you could possibly think of. You can also sign up for her newsletter and techie tip of the day.

seoegghead.com/ is a blog dedicated to search-engine optimization.

Webconfs.com is a free site where you can measure the effectiveness of your web site with the search engines.

INDEX

BONUS OFFER DETAILS

At eBoot Camp, we are constantly searching the Web for valuable Internet marketing resources to help our clients get an edge on their competition. These resources consist of keyword suggestion tools, SEO tips and suggestions, social networking sites, social bookmarking sites, article and press release submission sites, blogging tools, and so much more. To receive free access to my private vault of Internet marketing resources, go to www.ebootcampbook.com/resources and enter your name and e-mail address along with the access code: ***ebootcamp247*** and you'll be given immediate access.

Enjoy!

Corey